Ready to go!

IDEAS FOR CHRISTMAS

KS1

P1 to 3

AUTHOR
Moira Andrew

EDITOR
Alison Rosier

ASSISTANT EDITOR
Roanne Davis

SERIES DESIGNER
Anna Oliwa

DESIGNER
Paul Roberts

ILLUSTRATIONS
Lisa Williams

COVER ARTWORK
Andy Parker

Designed using Adobe Pagemaker
Published by Scholastic Ltd, Villiers House, Clarendon Avenue, Leamington Spa, Warwickshire CV32 5PR
Printed by Bell & Bain Ltd, Glasgow

1 2 3 4 5 6 7 8 9 0   1 2 3 4 5 6 7 8 9 0

British Library Cataloguing-in-Publication Data
A catalogue record for this book is available from the British Library.

ISBN 0-439-01855-2

Contents

Introduction

This book provides a resource bank of ideas for lessons on a Christmas theme for children from 5 to 7 years old. It includes a retelling of the first Christmas story and the stories and legends, poems and songs which have grown out of the events in Bethlehem. Many of the traditions and customs of Christmas are explored and their similarities and differences examined. Each activity examines one aspect of Christmas in detail.

A considerable amount of research has gone into this book and it is hoped that the information provided will enable teachers to interest and excite the children about many different aspects of this special time of year and the different ways in which Christmas is celebrated around the world.

Each of the six sections contains a set of related lesson plans. Each begins with a set of clearly stated objectives which provides the main learning focus of that lesson. The objectives range across the curriculum, to help you to plan a Christmas project that will give the children a variety of learning outcomes, not only in the obvious area of religious education but in language work, history, music and art activities. The objectives are followed by a number of other cross-curricular links that could be explored or emphasised. These are related to the main objectives but provide further ideas for ways in which the study of Christmas traditions can be built into everyday class work in the days and weeks leading up to Christmas.

Each lesson contains recommended resources for the main activity and suggests ways in which the children should be grouped. You will need to assess how many items are needed for practical activities depending on whether children are making things individually or in groups. It may sometimes be worth asking children to collect things like cardboard tubes or scraps of wrapping paper ahead of the session where they will be used.

The section on what to do provides detailed information about the activity and closely follows the stated learning objectives. Guidance is offered on suitable questions and expected answers. This section gives some information on customs and traditions and provides related stories and legends. It is intended that you should read aloud directly from the boxed text and encourage the children to make imaginative responses.

In many cases, ideas for differentiation are included at the end of the lesson plan to help you adapt the activities for children of varying abilities.

The Now or later suggestions are designed to encourage the children to explore and develop the topic. There are also many suggestions for related art and language activities and a number of ideas for display are offered.

Many of the lesson plans are supported by photocopiable pages, grouped at the end of the relevant sections.

Although the book is presented in a structured way, it is not intended that each lesson plan necessarily be followed to the letter. It is possible to use a 'pick-and-mix' approach in which various sessions are selected and built into a scheme of work for the winter term. Each lesson is discrete, so from time to time there is some overlap between activities. The sessions are designed to fit in with both whole-school and class projects while it is quite feasible to tackle each as a one-off Christmas theme.

Schools are rightly very concerned about the amount of time spent on activities associated with Christmas. However, with careful planning, the festival can be integrated into a well-balanced curriculum that can add to the enjoyment and understanding of children of every faith and culture.

The background information and the range of stories, poems and legends in this book will help you and the children to appreciate some of the many fascinating ways people around the world have of celebrating the Christmas festival, and will lead to greater insight into the traditions and customs of Christmas and the winter season.

This section looks at the way we prepare and look forward to Christmas – a period of great importance in the Christian calendar. This section explores the season of Advent, Mary and Joseph's journey to Bethlehem and the light and joy that Christmas brings to the dark days of winter.

STIR-UP SUNDAY

RESOURCES AND CLASSROOM ORGANISATION

You will need: a large current calendar; a selection of recipe books showing photographs of Christmas puddings; photocopiable page 11; the ingredients and kitchen equipment required to make Christmas puddings arranged on a low table.

Introduce the activity to the whole class. The puddings can then be made as a class or with the children in groups of about six (under the direction of one or more additional adults).

WHAT TO DO

First, look together at today's date on the calendar. Find St Andrew's day (30 November) and look for the first Sunday after that. Explain that this is the first Sunday in Advent and is when we are supposed to make our Christmas cakes and puddings. Ask the children why it is called 'Stir-up Sunday' and if they think it is a good name. Can they think of any others? (For example, *Mixing day, Make-a-cake day, Stir-and-steam day.*)

Show the children the Christmas pudding recipe on photocopiable page 11 and read it through. Help them to recognise and name the various ingredients. Let them smell the spices. Look at pictures of finished Christmas puddings and discuss what we have to do to transform the ingredients into a pudding ready for the table. Talk about the processes of weighing, mixing, steaming and so on.

Tell the children that Christmas puddings used to be made just from ground corn or wheat boiled up in milk and were called 'frumenty'. Over time, other ingredients such as prunes, currants, wine, spices, eggs and breadcrumbs were added to make the frumenty tastier. The puddings became known as 'plum porridge'. Point out that prunes are dried plums. People put in what they could find in the kitchen, even bits of beef and lamb.

Compare the ingredients in the original plum porridge with those in the recipe for a modern Christmas pudding. Weigh out the ingredients, mix them in a basin with a wooden spoon and show the children the resulting mixture. (This can be done either in groups or with the whole class. The recipe makes two puddings.)

Elicit from the children that the spoon is made of wood. It is said that the Christmas pudding mixture should be stirred only with a wooden spoon to remind us that Jesus was laid in a manger carved from wood. Another tradition says that we must stir 'sunwise', or 'clockwise' to follow the route of the Three Wise Men to the stable.

Tell the children a special prayer used to be said when the pudding was being mixed: *Stir up, O Lord, the wills of thy faithful people*. Discuss what this might mean, perhaps that we should try harder to do what God would want (or *will*) us to do? Ask the children to begin thinking about new prayers to be said on Stir-up Sunday.

Explain that everyone in the family used to be given an opportunity to stir the Christmas pudding mixture and make a wish. Let each child stir the mixture and make a wish before it is put into the basin to steam. (This takes several hours, so it will have to be done out of school time.)

OBJECTIVES

To enable children to:
- follow a recipe for Christmas pudding (English)
- learn about the tradition of Stir-up Sunday (history)
- consider how traditions change over time (history).

OTHER CROSS-CURRICULAR LINKS

RE
Thinking of a prayer for mixing the pudding and noting links between Stir-up Sunday traditions and the Christmas story.

ART AND DESIGN
Painting a picture of a Christmas pudding surrounded by the ingredients.

GEOGRAPHY
Tracing the route followed by the Three Wise Men on a map; finding out where spices and fruits are grown.

Tell the children that the pudding is often served on Christmas Day with flaming brandy on top. It is usually decorated with a red ribbon or a sprig of artificial holly. Sometimes there are charms hidden inside, rather like those found in crackers – a ring, a button, a five pence piece and so on.

Now or later

■ Bring in cooked puddings for children to taste if they wish. Ask them to describe the flavours, for example *like fruit cake, spicy and sweet, tastes like Christmas*. Make a wall dictionary of 'taste' words and phrases.
■ Encourage the children to make up new Stir-up Sunday prayers They might say, *Dear God, thank you for our Christmas puddings* or, *Dear God, help us to enjoy the special pudding we are mixing for your special day.*
■ On a map of the world, help the children to find the West Indies and other places that fruit and spices for the Christmas pudding come from. (Contact Schwartz Herbs & Spices, Thame Road, Haddenham, Aylesbury, Bucks, HP17 8LB for free information on spices.)
■ Ask the children to draw, paint and cut out Christmas pudding pictures. Suggest they make an 'opening' pudding with a flap to reveal the ingredients and charms inside. They can use crepe and tissue paper to make flames and sprigs of holly decorations on top Assemble the finished pudding pictures to make a frieze.

Getting ready for Christmas

Objectives
To enable children to:
■ understand the meaning of Advent (RE)
■ design and make an Advent calendar (D&T)
■ learn about St Thomas's day (history).

Other cross-curricular links
PSHE
Thinking about others; planning ahead; perhaps collecting for a children's charity.

Art and design
Making Christmas cards, wrapping paper and so on.

English
Writing a poem about the longest night in the year, 21 December.

Resources and classroom organisation
You will need: a calendar; an Advent calendar; books about making Christmas decorations and gifts, for example *Creative Christmas* by Joan Chambers and Molly Hood (Belair); photocopiable page 12 copied onto thin card; more thin A4 card; scissors; writing and drawing materials; glue; scraps of tinsel, ribbon, Christmas string and so on.

The children should work first as a class for listening and discussion, then in groups of about six.

What to do
Tell the children that *Advent* means *coming*. Long ago, in the Old Testament, the prophet Isaiah promised that, one day, a saviour would come into the world. Advent is the name given to the four weeks leading up to Christmas, when Christians get ready for the coming of Jesus, like when an extra-special visitor is coming to stay! This is when excitement begins to build up and we begin our Christmas preparations.

Talk about the things that different people need to do to get ready for the big day. Discuss how children might be able to help at home, for example decorating the Christmas tree, making and wrapping presents, helping to write cards, helping in the kitchen and so on. Look through the Christmas books with the children to find things they might like to make and do.

Talk about the special ways in which different families get ready for Christmas and how they build their own traditions. For example, some always put a holly wreath on the door, make cakes or trifles to an old family recipe, place particular decorations on the tree or always go to church on Christmas morning. Make sure that children of different faiths (or none) can make their own contribution.

Talk about things schools do before Christmas, such as rehearsing Nativity plays, practising carols and making decorations for the classrooms.

Explain that churches get ready to celebrate Christmas too. During Advent, they are often decorated with candles and branches of evergreen.

Tell the children about St Thomas's Day on 21 December, when we have the shortest day and the longest night. This is the day chosen by the church to encourage us to remember people less well off than ourselves. It might be a good opportunity to consider ways of collecting for children's charities.

In many countries, such as Germany, it is traditional to make an Advent wreath for the dinner table. Four candles are fixed on a base of holly sprigs or other evergreens. Sometimes ivy is twined through the wreath and it is decorated with shiny apples and fir cones. The candles are lit one at a time on each Sunday in Advent.

Look at the calendar and find 1 December, the first day of Advent. Show the children an Advent calendar and point out how it has numbered doors, 1–24. Demonstrate how one door can be opened each day to reveal a Christmas picture or a small sweet. Explain that they can start to use the calendar on 1 December and open one door only each day until Christmas Eve.

Tell the children that they are going to make Advent calendars. Some children will want to use the tree outline on photocopiable page 12, others might prefer to design their own (see Differentiation).

In groups, show the children how the doors are drawn on the top sheet of card, then ask them to cut them (on three sides only) so that they can be opened.

Help the children to glue the two sheets of card together around the edges, then ask them to draw a different Christmas picture behind each door. The calendar can be decorated with stars, scraps of tinsel or Christmas string

Let the children show their finished calendars to one another. Remind them that Advent, the four weeks before Christmas, is a time when Christians get ready to celebrate the birth of Jesus.

Differentiation

Some children may wish to create a different background for their Advent calendar. Discuss appropriate backgrounds, for example a church, a block of flats, a sailing ship, a plum pudding, a Christmas tree – any theme that can accommodate 24 opening doors. Some children may need help cutting open the doors.

Now or later

■ As a class, think about the longest night of the year and discuss 'dark' words, for example *black, deep, shadowy, spooky* and so on. Think of night-time images and write an image poem together, for example:

The longest night is like
    a deep dark river.
It is like a tall black tree
    in a shadowy forest.

■ Suggest developing the idea of St Thomas's day by putting on a play or collecting toys for children for whom Christmas may not be a very happy time.

■ Let the children look through some Christmas craft books and choose something to make that will help prepare for Christmas, for example wrapping paper made by printing with raw potatoes or bookmarks to give as presents.

■ Ask the children to make an Advent table wreath. They will need two potatoes; an apple corer; a foil plate; four candles; sprigs of evergreen; decorations such as apples, coloured baubles and fir cones. Tell them to cut the potatoes in half and use the apple corer to make one hole in each half, one for each candle. Stick the candles firmly into the holes and stand the potatoes on the foil plate. Push the sprigs of evergreen into the potatoes and arrange in a circle, covering the plate. Decorate with apples, fir cones and Christmas baubles.

Winter weather

Objectives

To enable the children to:
- learn about winter weather and how each season brings different weather (science)
- learn about the winter solstice (history)
- investigate how winter weather affects birds and carry out a bird feeding survey (science)
- consider ways of keeping warm (science).

Other cross-curricular links

History
Learning how Christmas came to be celebrated during the winter solstice.

PSHE
Thinking of others (animals, birds and people) who suffer in cold weather.

RE
Understanding that one aim of the Christmas festival in this part of the world is to bring light and joy to dark days in winter.

Design and technology
Constructing a simple bird feeder.

Maths
Counting in months, weeks and days.

PE
Making up a snow dance, miming snowball fights or building snowmen.

Art and design
Making a collage of children singing carols in the snow.

Resources and classroom organisation

You will need: a calendar; a selection of children's cold weather clothes (woollen hats, scarves, gloves and so on); photocopiable page 13 and the resources listed to make a bird tray or feeder; a bird reference book; paper; writing and drawing materials.

The children should work first as a class for listening and discussion, then in small groups for practical work.

What to do

Find today's date together on the calendar. Look for 25 December, Christmas Day. Count how many months, weeks and days there are until Christmas. Ask which season December comes in. Can the children think of some of the features of this season? Ask how they differ from those of other seasons.

Talk about how early it gets dark in winter and how we need to get up before it is light to be in time for school. In this country, Christmas comes when the days are short and there is little sunlight. Tell the children that the shortest day and longest night of the year takes place on 21/22 December and is called the winter solstice.

Explain to the children that nobody knows the exact date of Jesus' birthday, but 25 December was chosen because it is close to the winter solstice. This was a time when people long ago used to hold great feasts, build huge bonfires and dance around the flames in the hope that this would give back light and strength to the Sun in time for spring. We, in turn, celebrate the birth of Jesus by giving parties, having lots to eat and lighting candles.

Discuss how in December, spring seems a long way off and the weather is often bitterly cold. Discuss the kind of winter weather we can expect, including cold winds, frost, ice and snow. During December, ask the children to record each day's weather in words and pictures on a weather chart.

Show the children boots, woollen hats and gloves, and so on and talk about the kinds of clothes we need to wear to keep out the cold. Think about people who do not have warm clothes to wear or homes to go to and discuss how they must feel.

Discuss how winter weather affects animals and birds and why we need to feed birds in severe weather. Show the children the wild birdseed and nets of peanuts and suggest that breadcrumbs, sultanas and scraps of fat or suet would also be a welcome addition to birds' winter diet. Emphasise the need for providing fresh water, especially when natural sources become frozen.

Discuss ways of making a feeding tray or the best place from which to hang a feeder. Organise the children into groups to make bird feeding trays or bird feeders using photocopiable page 13.

Ask the children to think of ways of recording the birds that come to feed during December. What will they need to record? For example, date, time of day, type of bird and so on. Show the children the bird book and identify four or five familiar birds likely to visit.

Date	Time of day	Type of bird	Weather	What the bird ate
15 Dec	*10.30am*	*Blue tit*	*Sunny, frosty*	*Peanuts*

Differentiation

Some children may be encouraged to work out other ideas for a bird survey. For example, they could weigh visiting birds by hanging a net containing 50g of peanuts on a spring balance. When a bird like a sparrow or blue tit stops to feed, they should read the scale, using binoculars if necessary, and deduct 50g from the reading.

Less able children may need to record bird visitors in a very simple form, for example a tally chart.

Now or later

- Help the children make a winter solstice calendar by drawing 31 squares on an A4 sheet. The squares should be numbered before each one is coloured yellow and black to represent daylight and darkness each day. The amount of darkness should increase up to December 23, then gradually show more daylight (yellow) and less night (black) as it gets towards the end of the month.
- Help the children use a weather chart to work out how many days of ice, rain, wind, fog, snow and so on there were on the days leading up to the Christmas holidays. This information could be recorded on a bar chart and the results discussed.
- In PE, ask the children to mime some of the ways in which we move in the snow and on the ice. They could also mime building a snowman or having a snowball fight. Then encourage the children to pretend to follow the tracks of a bird or an animal and make this into a snow dance. Other children could play chime bars, bells and triangles to accompany the dance.
- On paper, ask each child to draw and paint his or her head and shoulders, almost filling an A4 sheet. The mouth should be wide open as though singing and the children can paint a bright woolly hat on top of their picture heads. Assemble the pictures in groups, collage-style, on dark blue backing paper and dab with blobs of white 'snow'. Add lanterns and label the frieze, *We wish you a merry Christmas!*

The journey to Bethlehem

Objectives

To enable children to:
- learn about Mary and Joseph's journey from Nazareth to Bethlehem (RE)
- understand that the story comes from the Bible (RE)
- contrast the preparations for Jesus' birth and the place where he was born with those for today's babies (history).

Resources and classroom organisation

You will need: a few new-baby cards and a selection of baby clothes; a range of illustrated Christmas story books, for example *The Christmas Story* by Sheila Moxley (Tango Books), *The Donkey's First Christmas* by Kimberley Parr, (Dempsey Parr) and many more; *A Child's Bible* retold by Shirley Steen (Pan Books); photocopiable page 14, enlarged or on an OHT for display.

The children should work as a whole class to listen to your reading and for discussion afterwards.

What to do

Show the children some new-baby cards and talk about new brothers or sisters in the family. Encourage comments from the children whose mothers are expecting babies in the near future.

Tell the children that you are going to read the beginning of the Christmas story. Before reading, explain that Mary and Joseph had to make a long journey from Nazareth to Bethlehem to pay their taxes and that Mary was expecting a baby very soon. Discuss how tired and worried she must have felt as she and Joseph set out on their long journey.

OTHER CROSS-CURRICULAR LINKS

RE
Listening to different versions of the Christmas journey, emphasising that it comes from the Bible and that Christians believe it is true.

GEOGRAPHY
Following the route from Nazareth to Bethlehem.

HISTORY
Discussing how taxes were paid in biblical times, looking at clothes of the time, and thinking about how people travelled.

PSHE
Learning about how we look after new-born babies.

ENGLISH
Retelling the story of the journey orally and in writing and pictures.

The journey was approximately 75 miles and must have taken Mary and Joseph several days. Can the children imagine walking that distance from their nearest town, with no roads, just dusty pathways full of thorn bushes and sharp stones, and with mountains to cross too?

Explain that we don't know if the weather was cold or warm. Ask the children to think about what Mary and Joseph might have taken with them for the journey, for example lots of water, bread and fruit. Suggest that Joseph might have wanted a stick to help him walk over the mountains or a spare pair of sandals. Discuss what kind of clothes they would need and ask where Mary and Joseph would sleep – perhaps in a tent or under the stars? Nobody really knows!

Read Luke chapter 2, verses 1–7 from *A Child's Bible* that tells of the journey. Ask the children to imagine Joseph, footsore and weary going around Bethlehem knocking on every door until the innkeeper saw how tired Mary was looking and said that they could stay in the stable for the night. And there Jesus was born.

Make sure the children know what a stable is and who usually lives there. Discuss why it wasn't a particularly suitable place for a baby to be born. Ask where mothers go these days when they are nearly ready for their babies to be born.

Now read the story of the journey as told in one of the other versions, for example *The Donkey's First Christmas*, which tells the story from the donkey's point of view. Encourage comparisons with the Bible version and discuss how writers find different ways to tell the same familiar story. Ask the children to imagine how Mary might have described her journey.

Go on to talk about preparing for the birth of a new baby. Look at the selection of baby clothes and discuss what else new parents would want. Compare today's things with those Mary and Joseph might have had. Look at the illustrations in the picture books and think about the kind of clothes worn by adults and babies in biblical times.

Ask the children to look at photocopiable page 14. Compare how comfortable the modern mother looks in a hospital bed, her baby in a cot beside her with the other new mother, Mary sitting in a dusty stable, her newborn baby Jesus lying in a manger, *no crib for a bed...*

DIFFERENTIATION

Encourage competent writers to make a diary of Mary's journey as she or Joseph might have written it and add illustrations. Less able children could draw a picture diary, without words.

NOW OR LATER

- Look at a map of the Bible lands with the children and help them to trace the route Mary and Joseph might have followed on the road from Nazareth to Bethlehem.
- Make a chart with the children showing different ways of travelling, from walking to riding on donkey, horse or camel, to cars, buses and other modern means of transport.
- Ask the children to design a 'welcome to the new baby' card to welcome Jesus into the world.

Name Date

Christmas puddings

Ingredients:
225g shredded suet
110g self-raising flour
225g brown sugar
225g breadcrumbs
225g sultanas
225g currants
1 teaspoon mixed spice
1 teaspoon ginger
1 teaspoon cinnamon
½ teaspoon nutmeg
1 apple, peeled and grated
2 tablespoons milk
2 tablespoons syrup
juice of 1 lemon

What to do:

1. Grease two 1.2l (2 pint) pudding basins.
2. In a bowl, mix together the suet, flour, sugar, breadcrumbs and spices. Add the fruit and stir in well.
3. Mix the milk, syrup and lemon juice together and stir them into the dry ingredients. Let the mixture stand for one hour.
4. Stir the mixture again and make a wish. Spoon the mixture into the two basins. Cover with greased kitchen foil and tie with string.
5. Steam the puddings for about 8 hours, topping up the pan with water, as necessary.
6. Allow the puddings to cool. Take off the covers and replace with fresh kitchen foil. The puddings can be stored for up to a month in a cool dry place.
7. Reheat by steaming for 2 hours, or remove the foil, cover with a plate and heat in a microwave according to individual instructions.

Name Date

Advent calendar

Name Date

Make a bird feeding tray

You will need:

- a plastic seed tray (approximately 25×35cm) with holes at each corner
- hardboard to cover the base, also with holes at each corner
- good quality string or twine
- birdseed and/or breadcrumbs.

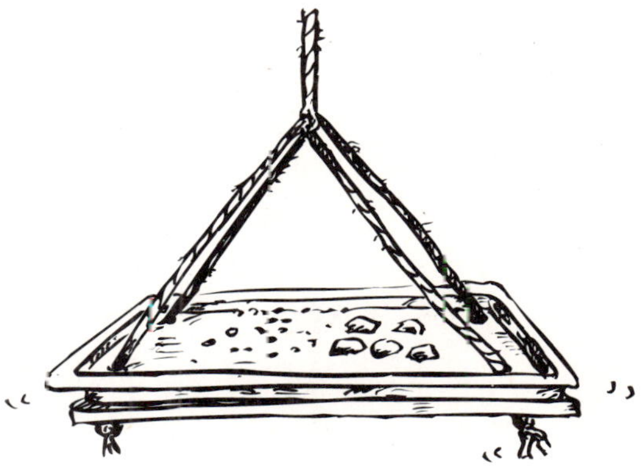

What to do:

1. Fit the hardboard into the base of the seed tray.

2. Thread a length of knotted string through each set of holes and fasten like a tent at the top.

3. Scatter birdseed or breadcrumbs on the tray and hang from a stout branch of a tree where it can be seen.

Make a bird feeder

You will need:

- a square piece of fine garden netting (approximately 30×30cm)
- an elastic band
- string
- unsalted peanuts.

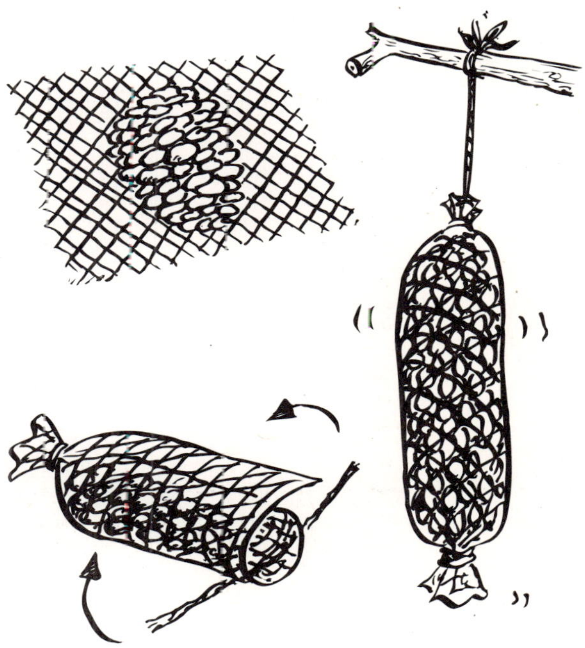

What to do:

1. Lay the square of netting on a flat surface. Place a good handful of peanuts in the middle of the netting.

2. Bring the corners of the bag together. Tie them with a piece of string or an elastic band.

3. Make a string handle for the feeder hang it from a branch.

Name Date

A child is born

This section tells the story of the first Christmas, followed by three Christmas legends. It offers an enjoyable listening experience and encourages the children to explore the difference between a legend and a true story.

The first Christmas

Objective

To enable children to: become familiar with the Christmas story (RE).

Resources and classroom organisation

You will need: a baby doll in a shawl; baby clothes; a few photographs of young babies; a selection of illustrated picture books about the Christmas story, for example *The Christmas Story* by Sheila Moxley (Tango Books), *The Christmas Story* by David Hately (Ladybird Books), *The Christmas Book* by Dick Bruna (Methuen).

Work with the children as a whole class for listening and discussion.

What to do

Talk about any new babies in the children's families. Ask them to describe what they look like, their size, name, what they do, what the children themselves do to help. Those who don't have a baby at home can choose a photograph to talk about.

Let the children hold the baby doll, stressing the care with which we must handle a new baby. Look at baby clothes and compare their size with the children's own.

Ask if the children can remember the name of the special Christmas baby. Tell them that you are going to read about the night Jesus was born. Use either an illustrated Christmas book or tell the story as outlined below.

Mary and Joseph had to make a long journey from Nazareth to Bethlehem to pay their taxes to the emperor Caesar Augustus. When Mary and Joseph arrived, the town was so busy that there was no room for them in the inn. The innkeeper said that they could sleep in the stable across the yard.

That night in the stable, beside the animals, Jesus was born. Mary wrapped him in a warm shawl and kissed him. There was no cot, so Mary put him in a manger, a wooden box filled with hay for the animals. Joseph lit the oil-lamp and he and Mary gazed down at their beautiful baby boy as he lay sleeping.

That night there were shepherds in the fields close by, keeping watch over their sheep. Suddenly, the sky was filled with angels, praising God. The shepherds watched in amazement. The angels told them that a baby called Jesus had been born in Bethlehem.

'This baby will bring joy to the world,' they said. 'You will find him in a stable, lying in a manger.' Then the angels vanished and the night sky looked blacker than ever.

The shepherds said to one another, 'We must go to Bethlehem to see this wonderful baby.' When they got there, they saw a bright star shining above a stable roof. 'This must be where the baby is,' they said. They went inside and there they found, Mary, Joseph and the baby Jesus, just as the angels had promised.

On the night that Jesus was born, Three Wise Men from the East saw a very bright star in the sky. From the books they had read, they knew that the star would lead them to a newborn king. They saddled up their camels and went on a long, tiring journey over mountains and deserts, through towns and villages.

At last they reached Bethlehem and saw the star above a poor stable. 'Is this the place where the baby is?' they asked one another. 'It doesn't look rich enough for a king!' They had brought presents for the baby, so they went inside where Jesus lay sleeping in the manger. One wise man brought gold another frankincense and the other brought myrrh. They told Mary that they had seen a bright new star and had followed it to where it stopped over the stable.

All over the world, people tell the story of the first Christmas and how a bright shining star led the shepherds and Three Wise Men to a stable in Bethlehem on the night that Jesus was born.

OTHER CROSS-CURRICULAR LINKS

HISTORY
Learning how Caesar Augustus ordered that everyone be taxed in the town of their birth.

PSHE
Looking after a tiny baby and knowing its needs.

ART AND DESIGN
Making a collage of the Nativity scene.

ENGLISH
Writing and illustrating a wall version of the Christmas story; performing a Nativity play.

Let the children have a few seconds of silent thinking time, then encourage them to explore some of the scenes in the story. Ask them to imagine a baby king being born in a stable with all the sounds and smells of the animals around. Discuss how Mary must have felt when she discovered that there was no bed for her baby. Ask the children to compare the things that Mary had with all the equipment that the babies they know have.

Talk about shepherds and their work and explore why they had to keep watch over their sheep all night long. Look at pictures of the angels and tell the children that angels are God's special messengers. Think about the wise men and explain that they were probably astrologers who thought that they could tell what was happening in the world by studying the stars.

DIFFERENTIATION

Encourage more articulate children to work on their own version of a Nativity play, making up the dialogue as they go along.

NOW OR LATER

- Help the children to make group collages of the Nativity scene using scraps of material to 'dress' the main characters.
- Make a wall version of the story in a zigzag format. Use simple sentences from the children's dictation, perhaps word-processed, and let each group paint a different scene to illustrate the story.

THE LITTLE FIR TREE

OBJECTIVES

To enable children to:
- know about Hans Christian Andersen, who first told the story of the Little Fir Tree (English)
- make up an alternative ending to the story (English/A&D)
- learn the difference between evergreen and deciduous trees (science).

OTHER CROSS-CURRICULAR LINKS

ENGLISH
Retelling the story orally and in writing; looking at more tales by Hans Christian Andersen.

PSHE
Thinking about why the little fir tree was unhappy.

DESIGN AND TECHNOLOGY
Designing and making Christmas decorations.

RESOURCES AND CLASSROOM ORGANISATION

You will need: a fresh sprig from a fir tree; a picture of a fir tree; a reference book on trees; pictures of Christmas trees; a book of Hans Christian Andersen's tales, for example *Favourite Stories from Hans Christian Andersen* edited by Andrew Matthews (Orchard Books); paper; writing and drawing materials.

Begin the lesson with the whole class, then the children work individually or in small groups.

WHAT TO DO

Let the children smell the sprig from a fir tree and ask them to describe its smell, for example *fresh, green, foresty, like the cold wind, Christmassy.* Tell the children that the sprig is from a fir tree and show them a picture. Explain that a fir tree is an evergreen and encourage them to work out what this means. Look in a tree recognition book for more evergreens and discuss why they make good Christmas trees.

Prepare the children to listen to the story, telling them that it was first told over a hundred years ago by a Danish writer called Hans Christian Andersen.

> Once upon a time, a small green fir tree grew in a dark forest. It was a very unhappy little tree and couldn't wait to grow tall and strong like its neighbours. In summer the Sun shone and the wind whispered in its branches. Birds nested in the little tree and squirrels ran up its narrow trunk but the little tree wasn't happy. 'If only I were a great big tree like the others,' it sighed.
>
> Sometimes in winter, when snow lay deep and soft on the ground, a hare came along and jumped right over the little tree. How it hated that! 'I wish I was big and tall,' it said to itself.
>
> By the time the little tree was three years old, it had grown so tall that the hare had to walk round it. But still the little tree wasn't satisfied. 'If only I could grow tall enough to reach the sky!' it thought.

One day in autumn, woodcutters chopped down some of the very tallest trees in the forest. The little tree asked the birds if they knew where the tall trees had gone.

'They have been taken away to make masts for sailing ships,' the birds said.

'I wish I could sail across the waves too,' said the little tree. 'What does the ocean look like?' he asked. 'Oh, it's big and wide and blue, very difficult to describe,' the birds said as they flew off.

Every year, just before Christmas, some of the fir trees were chopped down, so the little tree stood as straight and tall as it could, hoping to be chosen. But the woodcutters walked right past it. 'Where are these trees going?' the little tree asked

'We know!' called the sparrows. 'When we were in the town we locked in at the windows and you'll never guess... '

'Go on, go on,' said the impatient little tree.

'They stand the trees in a big red pot in the corner of the room and children decorate them with baubles and silver tinsel and lots of bright candles,' said the sparrows. 'Then the fathers climb up and place a shining star right on the top. You can't imagine anything so splendid!'

The little tree was so jealous that it wept great, fat tears. 'I wish they would take me to town and decorate me with baubles and candles,' it said. It went on feeling unhappy all through the spring and the summer and the autumn. It didn't enjoy the wind tickling its branches, the Sun beaming down and the birds nesting in its branches.

The little tree grew taller and taller, all green and fresh and beautiful. Everyone said, 'What a lovely tree!' and when Christmas time came, the little tree was the first to be cut down. It was so proud. 'I'm going to be a Christmas tree!' it called out to anything in the forest that would listen.

At last the little tree was taken into a big warm room. It was placed in a deep red pot full of sand. The little tree felt very excited. 'What's going to happen to me now?' it wondered.

Then three children ran into the room and began to hang golden apples, red baubles and little coloured boxes from its branches. Their mother placed lots of tinsel and candles all over the tree and their father put a huge silver star on top. 'We will light the candles as soon as it gets dark,' said the children's father. The little tree could hardly wait.

At last they lit the candles and the little tree stood shimmering in a blaze of light. 'I hope the sparrows are watching,' it said to itself as it admired its reflection in the window.

But Christmas was soon over and the children and their parents came to strip the decorations and pack them away in a box for next time. 'What's going to happen to me now?' the little tree wondered to itself. It found out soon enough. Next morning the tree was taken up into the attic and left in a dark corner.

The little tree was very lonely. It missed the birds and the squirrels, even the hare. 'I wish I was back in the forest,' it thought. It looked down at its bare branches as they began to turn brown. Now it knew what it was like to feel really unhappy.

But worse was to come. The little tree was dragged downstairs into the spring sunshine and the children's father came out and chopped it into little bits. He stacked them into one big bonfire and set it alight. It made a splendid blaze! As it burned, the tree sighed, remembering the Sun shining in the forest on summer days and snow falling like white rose petals in winter. It wished with all its heart that it had taken time to enjoy its life. Then, with one last sigh, the little fir tree was burned to ashes.

After a short 'thinking time', discuss with the children all the good things that had happened to the little tree. Ask why it wasn't satisfied. Talk about how the ending made the children feel.

Ask the children to draw and colour a happy ending to the story, for example the little tree planted in the garden, back in the forest with all its friends or as the tall mast on a sailing ship far out to sea.

Differentiation

More able children may be able to write their happy ending. They can also look at other stories written by Hans Christian Andersen to show the class, for example 'The Ugly Duckling'.

Now or later

- Ask the children to retell the story with a new, happy ending.
- With the children, make a list of some of the things that we use every day that are made out of wood.
- Think about why the people in the story lit candles on the tree. Discuss how dangerous this was and ask what we now use to light the Christmas tree instead.
- Use shiny or coloured paper to make decorations for the school Christmas tree. Tape string or cotton to the backs of the decorations to hang them with.

The legend of the spider's web

Objectives

To enable children to:

- understand what a legend is and that it is not necessarily a true story (English)
- learn about Herod, and Mary and Joseph's flight to Egypt (RE)
- appreciate some of the problems of refugees, then and now (PSHE).

Other cross-curricular links

Science
Observing spiders and understanding how they catch their prey.

Maths
Looking at the design of a spider's web.

Design and technology
Making a web with fine string.

Art and design
Drawing clothes and toys; making designs in silver on black.

English
Writing a poem from a story.

Resources and classroom organisation

You will need: *A Child's Bible* rewritten by Shirley Steen (Pan Books) – Matthew chapter 2, verses 12–16; illustrated books showing spiders and their webs, for example *Spiders* by Theresa Greenaway (Wayland) or *Collins Gem Spiders* by Paul Hillyard; paper; writing and drawing materials; scissors; glue.

Read the story to the class, then follow with activity work in small groups.

What to do

Ask the children if they know the story of the Three Wise Men who brought gifts for Jesus. Remind them that these men were astrologers, who studied the stars. Before the men arrived in Bethlehem, they went to see King Herod and told him that the stars had news of a newborn baby who would grow up to be King of the Jews. Herod was upset, but he pretended that he wanted to worship the new king and asked the visitors to return with news of where he could be found.

The Bible story tells us that, when the time came for the Wise Men to leave, they returned to their own country by a different route for they had been warned in a dream not visit King Herod again.

When Herod realised the Wise Men had tricked him, he was furious. He told his soldiers to look for and kill every boy child under the age of two in and around Bethlehem.

Then an angel came to Joseph in a dream and told him, 'Take Jesus and Mary to Egypt. You must stay there until I tell you to leave because Herod is going to try to kill Jesus.' So right away, in the middle of the night, Joseph set off for Egypt with Mary and the baby Jesus.

Tell the children that Christians believe that this story is true because they can read about it in the Bible. Show them the verses in Matthew where this part of the story is told.

Now suggest that a legend has been built up around the next part of the story. Explain that a legend is a made-up story, one that has been around for a long time, perhaps told from one person to another before it was ever written down. Read the next part of the story:

When Joseph and Mary and Jesus were on their way to Egypt, so the legend goes, they got so tired that they could go no further. Joseph searched for somewhere for Mary and Jesus to rest.
He found a deep, dark cave at the foot of a mountain. 'We can sleep in here,' he said. 'It's bitterly cold, but at least it's dry.'

Mary carried the baby into the cave and wrapped him up in a woollen shawl. The ground outside was freezing and white with frost. The cave was cold too so that the baby shivered and began to cry.

All the time, a little spider was watching. He heard the baby cry and saw how his mother cuddled him to try and keep him warm.

'I wish I could do something to keep this tiny baby warm on such a night, but there isn't much a little spider can do,' said the spider to himself. And then he had an idea.

'I know!' he thought. 'I can spin a web across the mouth of the cave. It will keep out the wind.' So the little spider got to work. Soon, a web, white with frost, hung like a silver curtain across the entrance. It wasn't quite so cold in the cave now, and Mary rocked her baby to sleep.

Just then, a platoon of Herod's soldiers marched along the path. They were looking for the boy babies that Herod had ordered to be killed. They stopped right outside the cave. Mary and Joseph held their breath, hoping that Jesus wouldn't wake up.

'Look,' said the soldiers' leader. 'There's a spider's web right across the entrance. It's not broken so there can't be anyone hiding inside. We must look somewhere else.'

So the soldiers went away and left the little family safe – and all because a little spider had spun a web across the mouth of the cave.

And legend says that is why, to this day, we put tinsel on our Christmas trees. The glittering silver strands remind us of the little spider's web woven across a deep, dark cave on the way to Egypt.

Encourage the children to think about the story for a minute or two, then discuss the difference between a true story and a legend.

Now explain that the holy family were refugees – people driven out of their own lands, sometimes because of war, sometimes because other people don't like them. How do the children think Mary and Joseph felt in the strange land of Egypt? What would they miss from home? Discuss how refugees coming to our country might feel. You may have children from refugee families in the class – encourage them to contribute if they would like to.

Ask the children to draw, colour and cut out the clothes and toys they would want if ever they had to leave home in a hurry, for example because of a flood. Help them to paste the cut-outs inside the outline of a suitcase and label everything for a display.

Now or later

■ Ask the children to look carefully at the design of a web in pictures, better still, outside on a frosty morning. To make its web, the spider first shoots out a thread of sticky silk which catches on a twig or a branch. Then it spins threads around the web and into the centre to make 'spokes'. Finally the spider makes a spiral beginning from the centre, latching his spider-silk onto the spokes as he spins.

■ Let the children make a web by dipping a piece of netting (from a fruit bag) in some starch. They should then paint the netting black and let it dry. Then, using silver string, help the chi dren thread eight spokes across the net. They will need to work from the middle out, adding a silver spiral to make a spider web design.
■ Write the story of the spider as a poem. Encourage the children to keep it simple and don't insist on rhyme. A rhyming example might go:

I am a spider, fat and black,
I live in a deep, cark cave.
Is that a baby's cry I hear?
This baby I must try to save!

Come inside, mother and child,
Come inside where it's warm.
I'll spin a web like a curtain
And I'll keep you safe from harm.

The birds' Christmas tree

Objectives

To enable children to:
■ learn about a traditional story from another country (English)
■ think about giving (PSHE)
■ find out about what kind of food is best to feed birds in the winter (science).

Other cross-curricular links

Geography
Understanding the location of Russia and the Arctic.

Science
Recognising the names of some common garden birds.

Design and technology
Constructing a simple bird feeder; making 'string treats' for birds.

Maths
Making a chart of the most common bird visitors to the school playground.

Art and design
Thinking of new ways to decorate a Christmas tree; painting a tree and birds.

Resources and classroom organisation

You will need: a map of Europe; paper for a wall chart; dried fruits, such as apricots, apple slices, dates, raisins, sultanas; skewers; string; lolly sticks (with a small hole made in the middle).

Read the story to the class then organise the children in small groups.

What to do

Tell the children that you are going to read a legend from Russia. First look for Russia, and the Arctic, on the map together and establish that the winters are extremely cold there.

Once upon a time, so they say, an old woman and her husband lived together in a cottage on the edge of a deep forest in Russia. They were very poor indeed and found it hard to buy enough food to keep themselves going.

Winter was always very cold but this particular winter was colder than anyone remembered. Snow fell for days on end and lay deep and white all around. The rivers froze and a biting wind blew down from the Arctic.

The old man said, 'I've never known such cold. I must gather lots of firewood to keep us warm.'

'Take care,' called his wife as the old man trudged off into the forest.

The old woman was kept busy cleaning and polishing the little cottage until it shone. Then she remembered the date, only a week until Christmas. 'We won't be able to afford a Christmas pudding this year,' she thought to herself. 'Nor Christmas cake, nor Christmas presents. It won't seem like Christmas, so it's not worth even thinking about a tree!' she sighed.

When the old man came back through the snow, dragging a big bundle of firewood, the old woman said,

'At least we will be warm inside our own little cottage. That's something to be glad about.' They threw logs and branches on the fire and flames leaped and danced in the hearth.

Just then, a knocking came at the window. 'Who can that be?' the old people asked one another. They had to melt a hole in the ice on the window to see out. They saw a group of robins and sparrows and thrushes huddled on the window ledge. 'Oh my poor feathered friends,' fussed the old woman. 'I've been so busy, I haven't fed you yet today.'

So she gathered the scraps left over from dinner and threw them to the birds. There wasn't a lot left, to be sure, but the old woman scattered as much food as she could find. Because the ponds and the streams were covered with ice, the birds had nothing to drink, so the old woman filled a saucer with warm water and put it on the window ledge too.

Every day, more snow fell until it drifted high up the cottage walls, covered the fence and weighed down the branches of the little tree standing alone in the middle of the garden. On Christmas Eve, the old woman had a good idea. 'Let's give the birds a Christmas tree of their own,' she said. So, instead of scattering crumbs on the window ledge, she tied scraps and sultanas and pieces of fat to the end of every branch of the little tree.

* * *

That night, it was so cold that the old woman and her husband sat wrapped in blankets round the dying fire and thought about all the Christmases they could remember. 'None ever as grim as this one,' they said. At the stroke of midnight, they heard the sound of church bells echoing across the forest. The old man kissed his wife's cheek, 'Happy Christmas, my dear,' he said.

On Christmas morning, the old people awoke to the sound of birdsong. 'Listen,' said the old woman. 'It sounds as though all the birds in the forest are singing!' She looked out of the window.

Frost and snow gleamed in the winter sunshine. In the middle of the garden stood the little snow-covered tree, its branches sparkling like strands of tinsel and on the end of every branch, in place of a glass bauble, a bird stood fluttering its feathers and singing at the top of its voice. 'Merry Christmas! Merry Christmas!' they all sang.

'What a marvellous present! It's going to be a wonderful Christmas Day after all!' the old woman said to her husband as they hurried outside to admire the Christmas tree that the birds had decorated – just for them.

Give the children a little time to reflect, then explore aspects of the story in more detail by asking questions such as: *What was the unusual Christmas present that the old couple received? Why do you think it made them so happy? If you could choose only one Christmas present, what would it be?* Discuss how the biggest and most expensive present is not necessarily the best. *How was the birds' Christmas tree decorated? Can you think of other ways to decorate a tree? How did the old woman look after the birds in cold winter weather?*

Ask the children to think about ways in which we can help feed birds in winter time, for example by putting out bread crusts, peanuts, bird seed, suet, dried fruit and so on. Remind them how important it is to provide water.

Make a wall chart of the most attractive foods, perhaps with the title *The Best Bird Restaurant in Town* or *Land here for your perfect Christmas meal!* Ask the children to think of more fun names for the wall display.

Show the children how to make 'string treats' for the birds. Each group should first thread a lolly stick 'perch' to sit at the end of a knotted length of string. They can then use a skewer to make holes in the dried fruit and thread four or five pieces onto the string.

Help them to hang the Christmas treats outside, on the lowest branches of a nearby tree.

Differentiation

Suggest that the most able children might use the RSPB website – www.rspb.org.uk – to find out more about feeding birds in wintertime. They should print out some of the information and discuss their findings with the other children in the group.

Now or later

- Let the children make simple bird feeding trays (see 'Winter weather' on page 8) and hang them near the classroom window.
- Use a bird book to help with recognition of common birds and make a chart to identify those that visit the bird feeders and the string treats most frequently.
- Let each child paint and cut out a colourful bird. They can then decorate it with sequins, scraps of tissue paper, feathers and so on. Ask each group to paint a bare tree with lots of branches and dotted with white or silver paint, to display their birds.
- The children could make a forest scene of black tree silhouettes and a cottage on a dark blue background. They could add white and silver paint or glitter for snow and some colour to show the cottage windows and door. Ask the children to cut out a Christmas tree to put in the garden and decorate, each branch decorated with a vividly coloured bird.
- Get the children to make a gift outline and to draw four Christmas presents for birds inside.

Section 3 Poems and songs

This section examines four Christmas songs and poems in depth and looks critically at the way in which they have been constructed.

The Twelve Days of Christmas

Resources and classroom organisation

You will need: calendars for both the current year and the next; 'The Twelve Days of Christmas' and the musical accompaniment, for example from *Carols for Choirs 2* edited by D Willcocks and J Rutter (OUP); an illustrated version of the poem, for example *The Twelve Days of Christmas* by Brian Wildsmith (OUP); a fresh pear, a 'gold' ring; pictures of a partridge, doves, hens, blackbirds, geese, swans and so on; percussion instruments.

The children should be seated as a class to start with, then in small groups.

What to do

Make sure the children know the dates of Christmas Day and New Year's Day and find them together on the calendar. Count 12 days forward from Christmas and show that this date falls on 6 January.

Tell the children that the Christmas holidays used to last from 25 December for 12 days. In those days, all holidays were 'holy days'. The church encouraged people to go to church and light a candle on each of the twelve nights between Christmas Eve and the eve of 6 January, Twelfth Night.

Go on to explain that, even today, our Christmas festivities finish on Twelfth Night. Explain that many people believe that all the decorations must be taken down by then or they will have bad luck throughout the year.

In medieval times, as well as going to church, people celebrated the twelve days of Christmas with fairs, feasting and dancing, night and day. Each day, they visited one another's homes and brought little gifts. Sometimes they brought sweets or cakes, sometimes fruit, or birds and animals that they had caught while they were hunting.

The song 'The Twelve Days of Christmas' tells us about some fantastic gifts that one lucky lady was sent each day from Christmas until Twelfth Night. Ask the children to listen while you read (or sing) the poem. Point out that the poem is cumulative, each verse adding on another number until 12 is reached.

Show the children the fresh pear and ask if they know where pears are grown. Then ask the children if they can remember all the birds in the song. Show them pictures of a partridge, hens, swans and so on. Explain that a 'colly bird' is a blackbird. In those days blackbirds and swans would have been eaten, just as we eat turkey today. Can they think of a nursery rhyme in which blackbirds were made into a pie? ('Sing a Song of Sixpence'.)

Suggest that with such a long holiday over Christmas, all the extra food would have been very welcome. The drummers and the pipers would have played for the singing and dancing that took place over the festive season.

Divide the children into six groups to recite 'The Twelve Days of Christmas', each group adding on their own verse so that it becomes a choral speaking piece.

Objectives

To enable children to:
- understand that in the past, Christmas celebrations used to last for twelve days (history)
- learn a traditional poem as a piece of choral speaking (English).

Other cross-curricular links

RE
Finding out how people believed that the twelve days of Christmas gave us time to think about coming closer to God.

Science
Recognising different birds.

History
Learning that people used to hunt for food for the festive season.

Art and design
Making a wall frieze of a song or poem.

Music
Singing a song; putting a percussion accompaniment to a song.

Now or later

■ 'The Twelve Days of Christmas' can be sung as a Christmas carol. The children can accompany the music with percussion instruments.
■ Show the children a gold wedding ring and discuss who wears one and what it means. Ask why the poet might have given his true love five gold rings.
■ Look at and discuss illustrations for 'The Twelve Days of Christmas', for example in the Brian Wildsmith book. Working in groups, ask the children to paint and cut out the pear tree and partridge, two doves, three hens and so on. Then use these paintings as the basis for a wall book with the appropriate number and picture for each of the twelve days.

Jingle bells

Objectives

To enable the children to:
■ enjoy listening to a well-known Christmas song (music)
■ become familiar with and sing 'Jingle Bells' (music)
■ use percussion instruments to accompany a song (music)
■ understand the importance of bells at Christmas (RE).

Other cross-curricular links

Science

Finding out about snow and the different ways of travelling across it.

English

Writing short image poems about snow.

PE

Practising snow-related movements and creating a 'snow' dance.

Art and design

Making snowflake patterns.

Resources and classroom organisation

You will need: 'Jingle Bells' on photocopiable page 29 and the musical accompaniment, for example from *Jingle Bells and Other Songs* edited by John Byrne and Anne Waugh (OUP) or a recording of 'Jingle Bells' and a tape or CD player; *The Snowman* by Raymond Briggs (Puffin Books); percussion instruments including, for example, Indian bells, finger cymbals and chime bars; pictures of snow scenes from books and cards.

If you are lucky enough to have a snow fall around Christmas time, get the children dressed in outdoor clothes and go outside for a few minutes to experience the magic of a fresh snowfall. Failing this, have the children seated as a class around the piano or tape player.

What to do

Sing 'Jingle Bells' or play it on tape to the children. Ask them if and when they have heard it before. Teach the words. Ask the children to make a picture of the song inside their heads. Discuss what time of year it is and what the weather is like.

Ask them to describe the picture they have made in their imagination. Look at snowy day illustrations, particularly of children playing. Ask them to think through the senses – how cold snow feels, how silently it falls, the noisy sounds of children playing in the snow, the taste of a snowflake on the tongue, how it changes the shape of familiar things around us, and so on. Talk with the children about the movement of falling snow and search for words to describe it, for example *whirling, swirling, dancing, feathering*. Make a list of snow words on the board.

Read *The Snowman* and ask the children to imagine holding hands with James and the snowman. Explore the idea of flying through the cold moonlit air. Emphasise the magical element of this story.

Now ask the children to listen to 'Jingle Bells' for a second time, suggesting that they join in as they become familiar with the words. Ask some questions to check on how well they have been listening, for example: *What does the song tell you about the way the children were moving? What do you think a 'one-horse open sleigh' would look like? What word tells you they were going fast? How did the children feel? Find some happy words in the song. Can you think of any more?*

Ask the children to think about the bells jingling on the horse's reins and explain that we often associate the sound of bells with Christmas. Tell the children that, if they are still awake on Christmas Eve, they may hear the church bells ringing at midnight to tell us that Jesus has been born. In Scandinavia, the church bells ring out at four o'clock on Christmas Eve so that people know that Christmas has begun and that they should stop work and go home.

Give out Indian bells and finger cymbals to some children and put a couple of children at the chime bars. Ask them to accompany the song with their instruments while the others sing the words. Give everyone an opportunity to play an instrument.

Now or later

- Ask the children to use simple reference books to find out all they can about snow, for example that it is made up of water, that newly fallen snow is brilliant white, that no two snowflakes have the same pattern and so on. Scribe a 'Snow science' sheet.
- Perform 'Jingle Bells' to an audience with some children singing and other children accompanying the song with a variety of percussion bells.
- Ask children to think about the way in which snow swirls to the ground and practise hand movements, then whole body movements to create a snow dance to the music of percussion bells.
- Show the children various pictures of snowflakes, emphasising their six-pointed star pattern. Give the children circles of white paper to fold into six equal parts before using safety scissors to cut out snowflake patterns. Display on deep blue or black frieze paper.

Differentiation

Invite independent writers to put together three-line images about snow, for example:

Snow is like
feathers
on a dove's wing.

Snow is like
daisy petals
scattered on the grass.

The poems can be displayed in a wall book, or ask the children to make zigzag poem books with a verse on each page. Alternatively, snow poems could be mounted on white circles, like snowballs. Children who have not written poems can make a collage of warmly dressed children throwing the 'snowballs'.

The Christmas Star

Objectives

To enable children to:
- recognise the importance of the Christmas star (RE)
- learn about the Three Kings or Wise Men (RE)
- learn a Christmas poem by heart (English)
- learn about the Polish tradition of Starboys (geography).

Resources and classroom organisation

You will need: photocopiable page 30; books about stars or pictures to show the main constellations; *A Child's Bible* rewritten by Shirley Steen (Pan Books).

Work with the children as a whole class.

What to do

Explore the feelings of excitement and anticipation associated with the arrival of a new baby, listening especially to those children who have had new brothers and sisters. Discuss the visitors who normally come to see a new baby in the family and the questions they ask, for example *What weight is she? What are you going to call him? Who does he look like?* and so on. Talk about the various gifts that a new baby often receives.

Tell the children that Jesus had special visitors who travelled a very long way to see him and take him presents when he was a new baby. These visitors didn't come by aeroplane or train or car. They travelled by camel! These were the Three Kings or Three Wise Men.

OTHER CROSS-CURRICULAR LINKS

SCIENCE
Looking at a constellation map and learning the names of familiar constellations.

HISTORY
Learning how people travelled in Biblical times and appreciating what an undertaking the journey to Bethlehem was for the Three Wise Men.

GEOGRAPHY
Following the route of the Three Wise Men on a map.

RE
Learning about the significance of gold, frankincense and myrrh.

ENGLISH
Listening to rhyming words and finding alternatives.

DRAMA
Dramatising the journey of the star.

DESIGN AND TECHNOLOGY
Making Christmas stars to dangle from sticks.

Remind the children of the part the Three Kings played in the Nativity story:

> Soon after Jesus was born, a party of astronomers came from the east, travelling towards Jerusalem and asking everyone they met, 'Where is the child that is born to be King of the Jews? We have seen his star in the east and are following it.'
>
> *(Matthew, Chapter 2, verses 1–2)*

Explain that the kings were astronomers. Elicit or tell the children that astronomers are people who know a lot about stars and the night skies. When these very wise men saw such a bright star one night, they looked in their books and read the prophecy that 'a king, like a bright star, will be born in Israel'.

Remind the children that the Three Wise Men brought Jesus gifts 'fit for a king' – gold, frankincense and myrrh. Tell the children that frankincense was a very expensive perfume, myrrh a rich ointment – both just as precious as gold.

The people of Poland still celebrate the Christmas star. People there fast on Christmas Eve until the first star lights up the night sky. Then they wish each other a happy Christmas and sit down to a special supper. Afterwards, the Star Man arrives and gives the children little presents. The children dress up as Starboys, each holding a lit-up star on a stick, and lead their parents into church for the midnight service.

Read 'The Christmas Star' on photocopiable page 30. Ask the children to listen to the story and 'see' the picture it paints, then take a quiet moment or two's reflection.

Ask questions such as: *What was the weather like? What word suggests that it was a very cold night? What was the journey like? Can you find words that tell us that the kings thought they had arrived at the wrong place? What happened next morning?*

Establish that the Three Wise Men had to go on a very long journey by camel. As the poem says, they went through different regions, *over sand and plain, up-hill, down-dale*, so they must have been very tired indeed when they arrived.

Read the poem again and ask the children to listen for the rhyming words: *sky/eye, trail/dale, shed/bed, sight/light*. Ask them to think of more words to rhyme with these.

Teach the poem line by line, slightly exaggerating the rhyming words, so that the children find it easy to learn by heart.

DIFFERENTIATION

Some children may wish to find out or imagine some different ways people travelled in biblical times, for example on foot, by donkey, by camel, in boats and so on. The class could make a travel map to show travel from biblical times until today. Some children could cut out or draw pictures for the map, while more able children could write a sentence or two of explanatory text beneath each picture.

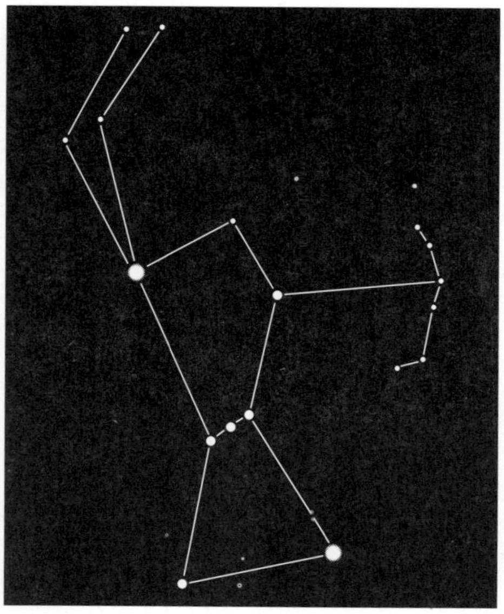

NOW OR LATER

- Look at some of the shapes of familiar constellations, for example Orion and the Great Bear, in the books about stars.
- The Wise Men travelled from Babylon to Jerusalem and on to Bethlehem. Help the children to follow their probable route on a contemporary map of the Holy Land.
- Let the children make stars to dangle from sticks like the Starboys of Poland. Provide star shapes in card for them to paint, colour and decorate.
- Dramatise the story of the Christmas star in words and music.

Away in a Manger

Resources and classroom organisation

You will need: an assortment of birth congratulations cards; photocopiable page 31; a cradle or baby's crib; a greengrocer's box filled with straw or hay; coloured paper or card; writing materials.

Have all the children seated in the story corner first, then working in small groups.

What to do

Look at the birth congratulation cards and discuss the occasion they celebrate. Talk about the joy and excitement of having a new baby in the family.

Remind the children of Mary and Joseph's journey to Bethlehem and what happened when they arrived:

When Joseph and Mary got to Bethlehem, they looked everywhere for a place to stay. But the town was full and there was no room at the inn, so they had to sleep in a stable. There, in the night, Mary's baby was born. She wrapped him up and laid him in a manger.

Discuss how Mary and Joseph were turned away from the inn and how they might have felt. Establish that a stable is a place where animals sleep. Ask them to suggest the kinds of animals who shared their home with Mary and Joseph, for example sheep, a cow and a donkey with perhaps doves and pigeons on the rafters. Can the children think of the noises the animals would make, how warm their breath would be and what the smell would be like.

Read the first verse of 'Away in a Manger' on photocopiable page 31. Then sing or play it so that the children can become familiar with the tune. Invite them to rock a pretend baby in time to the music and join in with the words as they get to know them. Explain to the children that this carol is like a lullaby – a song that helps to lull a baby to sleep.

Remind the children of the words, *no crib for a bed*. Can they remember where Mary put Jesus down to sleep? Tell them that a manger is where the animals' hay and straw is kept. Let the children look at and handle the baby's crib and compare it with the straw-filled box or 'manger'.

Ask the children to listen to the words of the next verse. Explain the meaning of *The cattle are lowing* (the cows are mooing) and ask the children to describe the other animal sounds. Explain that the word *nigh* is an old word for *near*, so the song is asking Jesus to look after children all through the night, until it is nearly morning. Sing or play this verse again, getting the

Objectives

To enable children to:
- learn that the first Christmas crib was said to have been set up by St Francis of Assisi (RE)
- learn and sing a well-known children's carol (music)
- appreciate that some babies are born to homeless families (PSHE)
- write prayers to make a 'prayer tree' (RE/English).

Other cross-curricular links

Music
Using percussion instruments.

English
Identifying rhyming words and finding new ones; writing a third verse for 'Away in a Manger'.

Drama
Dramatising a nativity scene from the words of a carol.

Art and design
Designing a card for the baby Jesus.

children to join in when they can. Tell the children that the last four lines are a prayer asking Jesus to love and care for children everywhere.

Explain that all over the world, people set up Nativity scenes in churches, in schools, under their Christmas trees and even outdoors in streets, shopping centres and market squares. The figures of Mary and Joseph, the ox, the ass, the shepherds and their sheep and the three kings are shown grouped in worship around the baby Jesus who is lying in a manger. Sometimes the figures have been carved from wood or are fashioned in clay.

St Francis of Assisi is said to have organised the first Nativity play in his church in 1224. He had a wax doll specially made to represent Jesus, and, to bring the scene to life, he hired actors to play the parts of Mary, Joseph, the kings and the shepherds and introduced real animals to the scene. Today, Nativity plays are performed in schools and churches each Christmas. 'Away in a Manger' is the carol most often sung at the end of the play.

To finish this session, draw the children's attention once more to the phrase, *no crib for a bed* and encourage them to think about what it must be like to have no home to go to, no roof above your head, no bed to sleep in. Invite them to think of simple prayers for homeless children and write them out on strips of coloured paper. These can be hung on a small artificial Christmas tree to make a 'prayer tree'.

Differentiation

Independent writers may enjoy making up a new third verse for 'Away in a Manger', for example:

> Love us, dear Jesus
> all day and all night,
> Morning and evening,
> in darkness and light.
> Thank you, dear Jesus
> for giving us food,
> For sunshine and moonshine
> and making us good.

Now or later

- Ask the children to note the rhyming words in the carol. See if they can find new rhyming words for *bed/said*, *lay/hay* and so on.
- Ask the children to accompany 'Away in a Manger' with percussion instruments. Choose triangles, bells and chime bars, played very softly.
- Ask the children to design a birth congratulations card for the baby Jesus, welcoming him to the world.
- Following the words of the carol, dramatise the Nativity scene. The shepherds and kings can form a tableau while angels sing 'Away in a Manger'. Mary rocks the baby to sleep and Joseph holds a lamp on high.

Name Date

Jingle bells

Dashing through the snow
In a one-horse open sleigh,
O'er the fields we go,
Laughing all the way.
Bells on bob-tail ring,
Making spirits bright.
What fun it is to ride and sing
a sleighing song tonight.

Jingle bells, jingle bells,
jingle all the way.
Oh, what fun it is to ride
in a one-horse open sleigh.
Jingle bells, jingle bells,
jingle all the way.
Oh, what fun it is to ride
in a one-horse open sleigh.

Now the ground is white
Go for it while you're young.
Take the girls tonight,
And sing this sleighing song.
Get a bob-tailed bay,
Two-forty for his speed.
Then hitch him to an open sleigh
And *Crack!* you'll take the lead.

Name Date

The Christmas star

A star looked down
from the frosty sky,
saw three lost Kings
and winked its eye.

"Follow me," it said
and blazed a trail
over sand and plain,
up-hill, down-dale.

It stopped at Bethlehem
above a poor shed.
"Here?" asked the Kings.
"The Child has no bed."

"Here," said the star
and faded from sight,
as sun bathed the Baby
in clear morning light.

Moira Andrew

Name Date

Away in a manger

Away in a manger,
no crib for a bed,
The little lord Jesus
laid down his sweet head.
The stars in the heavens
looked down where He lay:
The little Lord Jesus,
asleep in the hay.

The cattle are lowing,
the baby awakes,
But little Lord Jesus,
no crying he makes.
I love Thee, Lord Jesus!
Look down from the sky,
And stay by my side,
until morning is nigh.

This section examines the way in which Christmas is celebrated in other countries. The children are given opportunities to learn about the origins of the Father Christmas tradition and the importance of gift-giving in every Christmas tradition.

FATHER CHRISTMAS OR SANTA CLAUS?

OBJECTIVES

To enable children to:
- realise that the idea of Father Christmas or Santa Claus developed from the tradition of St Nicholas and the legend of Odin (history)
- appreciate that Christmas is celebrated in similar but different ways around the world (geography)
- understand that gift-giving is an important part of every Christmas tradition (RE/PSHE).

OTHER CROSS-CURRICULAR LINKS

HISTORY
Listening to old legends and learning how they have been transformed.

GEOGRAPHY
Finding out where The Netherlands and Lapland are on a map or globe.

RE
Thinking of the tradition of bringing gifts at Christmas.

DESIGN AND TECHNOLOGY
Making simple Christmas gifts.

ENGLISH
Making up four-line poems.

RESOURCES AND CLASSROOM ORGANISATION

You will need: Christmas cards and books showing different artists' interpretations of Father Christmas; wooden clogs or pictures of them; paper; writing materials.

Keep the children together to introduce the topic, then ask them to work individually or in small groups.

WHAT TO DO

Talk about children's images of Father Christmas, for example *quite fat, a long white beard, wears a red cloak* and so on. Encourage them to describe how Father Christmas is supposed to travel, where he lives, what he brings to the children of the world. Explore the magic and mystery in these ideas by asking questions like: *How do you know Father Christmas rides on a sleigh? ...carries presents in a sack? ...wears a red cloak? Have you ever met him?* Look at old Christmas card pictures and books about Father Christmas.

Tell the children that all over the world there are traditions of 'gift-bringers' – people who visit children and bring them presents at Christmas time. The one we know best is Father Christmas or Santa Claus.

Explain that children in The Netherlands believe that St Nicholas brings their Christmas presents, not on our Christmas Day but on 6 December, St Nicholas's Day. Tell them that the Dutch word for St Nicholas is *Sinterklaas*. Encourage them to say it quickly and they will soon see how it evolved into our *Santa Claus*. St Nicholas is supposed to wear a white cloak and a tall red hat. He doesn't travel in a reindeer-drawn sleigh but rides a white horse. Tell this Christmas story from Holland:

Christmas comes early in The Netherlands. On the night of 5 December, Wilhelm and Kjerste climbed the stairs to bed. For them, it was Christmas Eve, and it was starting to snow. They went upstairs slowly and carefully, each holding an old-fashioned wooden clog in one hand, a fistful of hay in the other. They were very excited and Kjerste was sure she wouldn't be able to sleep.

'Take care. Don't drop the clogs!' called their mother. 'They once belonged to your grandfather, remember!'

'I know,' Kjerste said impatiently. She showed her brother how to stuff his clog full of hay. 'Like this,' she said, making sure that the hay was pushed down right to the toe. 'On Christmas Eve every Dutch child does this, even Grandfather when he was a boy!'

'Why?' asked Wilhem.

'For St Nicholas's horse, silly!' said Kjerste.

'Well, I don't believe in that old story,' scoffed Wilhelm. 'How could anyone ride a horse through the sky in a snowstorm?'

'St Nicholas can!' said his sister. Their mother came upstairs. 'St Nicholas won't forget us, will he?'

'Of course not,' said mother. 'Put the clogs out on the window ledge, so that

St Nick's horse will find them. Then the good St Nicholas will come down the chimney with a present for you. Now, get into bed and I'll tell you a story.' She tucked the children under their duvets and sat on the edge of Wilhelm's bed.

'Once upon a time,' she began, 'long before anyone we know was alive…'

'Even before Grandfather?' asked Wilhelm.

'Yes, many, many years before that!' Mother went on. 'About four hundred years after Jesus was born, in the town of Myra, far away in Asia Minor, there lived a man called Nicholas. He was so good to everyone he met that all the people grew to love him and they made him a saint. Soon he became everyone's favourite saint.

In the town of Myra, so the legend says, a father lived alone with his three daughters.

Their mother had died. They were so poor that they scarcely had enough food to eat and the father could not afford dowries for his daughters.'

'What's a dowry?' asked Kjreste.

Her mother explained, 'A dowry is money a bride sometimes has to give her husband's family to get married. St Nicholas wanted to help these poor people but without anyone finding out. So, when the oldest daughter was old enough to get married, St Nicholas rode on his white horse to their cottage in the middle of the night. He climbed on to the roof and dropped a bag of gold down the chimney. It fell into the hearth.'

'Just like our presents!' said Kjreste.

'Just like your presents!' agreed mother. 'St Nicholas left a bag of gold on the hearth for each of the other daughters when they became old enough to marry. But on the night he brought the youngest daughter's gold, their father heard a horse whinnying outside the kitchen window. He jumped out of bed to see who was there. Imagine his surprise when he found St Nicholas astride a white horse, ready to ride away.

'Stop!' he called, 'How can I thank you, my friend?'

'You can thank me by keeping my visits a secret,' St Nicholas said.

So the father promised he would. And ever since, on 5 December, St Nicholas climbs on his white horse and rides secretly through the night to leave presents on the hearth for all the children of The Netherlands.'

By this time, Kjreste and Wilhelm were almost asleep. There was a sound of muffled hoofbeats on the snow-covered cobbles outside. 'Is that St Nicholas?' asked Wilhelm sleepily. 'Yes, I expect so,' said his mother as she went quietly downstairs to get ready for Christmas Day.

Next morning, before it was light, Wilhelm went to the window. Grandfather's old wooden clogs were empty. 'Wake up! Wake up, Kjreste!' he called. 'St Nicholas has been! His horse has eaten all the hay!'

'I told you so!' said Kjreste as they went to see what presents St Nicholas had left for them on the hearth.

'But I don't expect it's a bag of gold!' said Wilhelm – and it wasn't.

Give the children a few moments to think, then show them a pair of clogs if possible, explaining that they used to be the shoes worn by everyone in Holland. Let them handle them to see that they are made of wood.

Tell the children that the name *Father Christmas* might have come from another legend, this time from Lapland. In this story, Odin, known as 'The Old Man of the Snows' was, like St Nicholas, a gift-bringer. He was said to be a white-bearded old man in a blue hood who rode through the midwinter skies on a fast horse called Sleipnir. This Old Man of the Snows brought his gifts to cheer the people in the cold dark days of winter. They were so excited to see him that they opened their doors and ran out into the snow, calling out, 'Welcome, Old Father Christmas!'

Discuss these legends and traditions with the children, encouraging them to look for similarities and differences between these stories and Father Christmas as we know him today. Point out that all the Father Christmas figures are gift-bringers. It is through the giving and receiving of gifts that we can see the spirit of Christmas.

Together, think of gifts the children could give very easily. For example, they could give promises, perhaps to their parents or brothers and sisters, such as *I promise to tidy my bedroom*, or *I promise to share my toys with you*. Discuss their ideas and ask them to write out a promise. Display a banner of Christmas promises on the wall.

Differentiation

People in The Netherlands make up riddles about the gifts they are giving. Independent writers could make up short riddles in the same way. For example:

Guess what I am, golden and bright,
hoping you'll cuddle me every night.
No, not a toy lion but you're nearly there –
I'm a dear little teddy bear!

Other children could draw or paint gift ideas.

Now or later

■ Help the children to find The Netherlands and Lapland on a globe or in an atlas.
■ Many churches and schools organise a gift service for people to offer gifts for refugee children or for elderly people who have no one to visit them. It might be possible to arrange visits to local organisations, for example a home for the elderly, with small gifts that the children have made. Talk about the kind of Christmas gifts children could make, for example no-cook sweets, bookmarks, plant pots and so on. Alternatively they could collect unwanted toys and books.

St Lucy's Day

Objectives

To enable children to:
■ appreciate that there are different Christmas traditions in different parts of the world (geography)
■ learn that St Lucia (or St Lucy) is the patron saint of Sweden (history)
■ understand the importance of candles at Christmas (RE)
■ think about helping others (PSHE)
■ make biscuits using a recipe (D&T).

Resources and classroom organisation

You will need: a variety of lights (or pictures of them), for example lamp, torch, electric light bulb, fairy lights; a candle; matches; a calendar; photocopiable page 38 and the ingredients and equipment for Pepparkakor biscuits.

Introduce the story of St Lucy to the whole class, then divide the class into small groups (with adult support).

What to do

Show the children the collection of lights and ask them to suggest lights that are particularly associated with Christmas, for example stars, candles, Christmas tree lights, brightly lit shops, street decorations and so on. If possible, close the blinds and light the candle. Encourage the children to observe how just one tiny flame can light up the room.

Tell the children that, just like the candle, Jesus was described as 'a light in a dark world' and that is why we like to use lots of lights at Christmas when the winter days are short and the nights are long and dark.

Look at the calendar with the children and find 13 December together. Tell them that in Sweden, this is when the Feast of St Lucia, now usually called St Lucy, is celebrated. It used to be celebrated as a festival of light on the day they thought was the shortest and darkest day of winter. (We know now that 21 December is that day.)

Tell the children the story of St Lucia:

Many years ago, there was a young girl called Lucia who lived in the city of Rome where the cruel emperor had threatened to kill all the Christians.

The Christians fled into hiding. Some escaped to live in church cellars where they lived like rats in damp caves. Lucia, who was a very kind and thoughtful girl, hated to think about these poor men, starving themselves to death deep under the ground. She wondered what she could do to help. She decided to take food to them and saved every piece of fruit and crust of bread she could find.

When no one was looking, Lucia crept out into the streets and into the empty church. She tiptoed down the long stairs to the dark cellar. So that she could see in the darkness and still keep her hands free to carry the plates of food, Lucia tied a ribbon on her head and stuck lighted candles round it.

The starving Christians were delighted to see her and gobbled up the food she brought. She saved the lives of many Christians, all of whom were tremendously grateful to her.

A festival of light had been held since ancient times on 13 December in Sweden.

To remember Lucia's bravery, she was made a saint and the festival of light was changed into the feast of St Lucia, or St Lucy as she is now called. It is still a mystery how this girl from Rome came to be regarded as the patron saint of Sweden.

Tell the children that early in the morning, on 13 December in Sweden, one of the daughters of the family puts on a long white dress with a red sash. On her head, she places a crown of green leaves with five candles round it. Long ago, the candles used to be made of wax, but nowadays, for safety, battery-powered ones are used.

Then the girl creeps downstairs and carefully sets out a tray with coffee and saffron buns. She takes the tray up to her mum and dad who have to stay in bed until they hear their daughter coming in with their breakfast. Sometimes she sings a special St Lucy song. Afterwards all the family comes down to breakfast in a room that is brilliantly lit, using every candle and lamp in the house.

Now every village and town, every school and supermarket and every office and factory has its own St Lucy too. The official town St Lucy visits hospitals and children's homes, taking small gifts of Pepparkakor biscuits or saffron buns.

OTHER CROSS-CURRICULAR LINKS

PSHE

Thinking about ways of helping in the home, making and sharing traditional biscuits.

DESIGN AND TECHNOLOGY

Making an Advent crown.

Tell the children another legend about St Lucy:

> This legend comes from Varmland in Western Sweden. It tells the story of a young woman wearing a white dress with a bright red sash, with a crown of lights around her head. Early one morning, she appeared out of the winter mists aboard a sailing ship. Her crown of lights flickered and danced in the grey light of dawn. The people of the lakeside villages, who were very hungry after a long, hard winter, saw that the ship was laden down with delicious food. 'Help us, please help us. We are starving!' they called to the young woman in the white dress. The ship sailed close to the land and the woman gave all the food to the hungry people who had gathered on the shore. They thanked her and called her 'The Lady of the Lake'. She too, is still remembered in Sweden on 13 December.

Explain that the two stories have become mixed up as they have been told down the years so that the Lady of the Lake and St Lucia of Rome are now both called St Lucy, and her day of light is celebrated on 13 December.

Discuss with the children how the girl who plays St Lucy helps to look after her mum and dad and relate this to Mother's Day. Ask them to suggest some of the special things they try to do then, for example making breakfast, giving mum a posy of flowers, making or buying a little gift. Talk about something special that they might be able to do today to help mum and dad at home.

In small groups, and with adult supervision, ask the children to make Pepparkakor biscuits (see photocopiable page 38). These can be pierced near the top with a skewer before they cool down and later, threaded with cotton and hung from the Christmas tree.

Differentiation

Make a display of cookery books, open at pages showing biscuit recipes. Ask less able children to list as many different biscuit recipes as possible. Others could design packets for each kind of biscuit.

Now or later

- Let the children make an advent crown from twisted wire and green leaves. They can make white 'candles' to stick around the crown from rolled paper topped with brightly-coloured red crêpe 'flames'.
- Tell the St Lucy story at assembly, ending with a parade of girls dressed as St Lucy, perhaps offering the other children some freshly baked Pepparkakor biscuits.

Christkind

Objectives

To enable children to:
- examine some popular German and Austrian Christmas traditions (RE)
- think about how the coming of the Christkind brings whole families together (RE/PSHE).

Resources and classroom organisation

You will need: a map or globe to show Germany; an angel outfit; paper; writing and drawing materials; scissors; glue.

The children should be gathered together in the story corner, then in their classroom places.

What to do

Show the children where Germany is on a map or globe. Tell them that the German name for the baby Jesus is Christkind, meaning Christ Child. German children believe that the Christkind brings them presents of apples and oranges, nuts, sweets and sugar plums. He is said to have golden wings and be dressed in a white robe and wear a shining crown.

Sometimes, Christkind sends his messenger, Christkindl, instead. She is the Christmas angel, a beautiful fair-haired girl with flickering candles on her head. She is a gift-bringer and brings her presents in a basket. Now read to the children:

> In Germany, it is traditional on Christmas Eve to lock the room where the Christmas tree stands. Children are not allowed in and must go to bed early. When the church bells ring out at midnight, the children are wakened and dressed in their party clothes. They rush downstairs to look at the tree that is lit with strings of bright white lights. They are always just too late to catch the Christkindl but they know she has visited because lots of small presents have been spread out around the tree. Then, everyone in the family sits down at the table and more little surprise presents are exchanged. Some of the presents are home-made but everyone pretends that they have come from the Christkindl, or Christmas angel.

Ask the children to describe how they imagine an angel looks. Dress a child up as an angel and discuss whether he or she looks like the children's images of an angel. Compare this with pictures of angels. Explain that they are said to be God's messengers. Can the children remember where angels played important parts in the Christmas story? (Telling Mary about the baby Jesus and telling Joseph about Herod.)

Encourage the children to think and talk about all the family members who might like to take part in a Christmas Eve supper like those in Germany. They may wish to include friends, neighbours, favourite book or television characters and even the Christkindl or Father Christmas. Ask them to draw a plan of their Christmas table at home, making sure that they have a place for everyone with whom they would like to share the meal. The children can then draw and cut out all the Christmas treats that they would most like to eat – turkey, potatoes and gravy, trifle, Christmas pudding, mince pies, sweets and so on. They can label these and glue them onto the table plan.

Differentiation

Ask independent writers to design and write invitations to the Christmas Eve supper.

Now or later

- Compare German and British Christmas traditions.
- Let the children make some small Christmas gifts, for example bookmarks, finger puppets, no-cook sweets and so on.
- Ask the children to design Christmas wrapping paper. They can cut out small Christmas motifs such as stars, trees and stockings from old cards and use them to make wax crayon rubbings of these on white tissue or kitchen paper. Encourage the children to wrap, as neatly as possible, small presents (either ones they have made or things like pencil sharpeners, hair baubles or coins) in their paper.
- Finish off the session by reading *Little Angel* by Geraldine McCaughrean (Orchard Books) or another Christmas story that features an angel.

Other cross-curricular links

PSHE
Thinking about family relationships.

Art and design
Drawing a table layout and foods designing and printing Christmas wrapping paper.

Design and technology
Making and wrapping tiny Christmas presents.

Name Date

Pepparkakor biscuits

Ingredients:
400g plain flour
1 teaspoon bicarbonate of soda
2 level teaspoons each of ground ginger, ground cloves and cinnamon
230g soft margarine
230g dark brown sugar
3 egg whites
250g (approx) icing sugar

What to do:

1. Sift flour, spices and bicarbonate of soda into a bowl.

2. In another bowl, cream the margarine and sugar until light and fluffy, then beat in the egg whites.

3. Slowly work in the dry ingredients.

4. Wrap the dough in foil and chill for several hours.

5. Heat the oven to 180°C.

6. On a floured board, roll out dough to the thickness of a pound coin.

7. Cut it into shapes using biscuit cutters.

8. Place the shapes on an ungreased baking tin, leaving space between each.

9. Bake for 10 to 12 minutes.

10. Use a skewer to pierce the biscuits while they are still hot if you wish to make tree decorations.

11. Cool them on a wire rack.

12. Blend the icing sugar with the third egg white until it is stiff enough to pipe across the biscuits.

12. Ice wavy patterns across the biscuits and leave to set.

13. Thread the tree decorations with cotton and hang in place.

This section considers some of the rich traditions of Christmas and looks at the history behind them. It also provides children with the opportunity to make Christmas gifts and decorations.

CHRISTMAS TREES

RESOURCES AND CLASSROOM ORGANISATION

You will need: illustrations and photogaphs of decorated Christmas trees; a fresh sprig from a fir tree; a tree identification book, for example *Trees and Leaves* edited by Ingrid Selberg, Su Swallow and Margaret Stephens (Usborne); a small artificial fir tree; a string of tree lights.

Children should be seated in the story corner as a class.

WHAT TO DO

Look at pictures of Christmas trees with the children. Ask if anyone knows the name of the tree that we bring into our houses at Christmas time. Let the children handle the fresh fir tree sprig. Ask them to describe its smell. Help them find the picture of a fir tree in the tree identification book and tell them that it is called an *evergreen* tree. Discuss with the children what *evergreen* means and help them find other examples of evergreens in the book. Mention that trees that drop their leaves are called *deciduous*.

Tell the children that nobody really knows who first thought of a Christmas tree, but we do know that the modern tradition came from Germany.

There are many legends about how fir trees came to be at the centre of our Christmas celebrations. One ancient legend says that a very holy man called St Boniface was sent from England to Germany to teach the people about Jesus.

One winter night, he and his monks were praying together in the woods when they saw a group of villagers getting ready to sacrifice a little boy to the god, Odin. They had tied the boy to an oak tree, but Boniface was just in time to save him. He chopped the oak tree down and, as it toppled to the ground, it left behind a little fir tree that had been growing among its roots.

St Boniface told his monks to put their candles on its branches and the little fir tree twinkled and sparkled in the dark. Then he turned to the people and said, 'From now on this little tree will be a sign of peace. Its evergreen leaves will remind you of Jesus. We will call it the tree of the Christ Child.'

Another legend tells us that on the night Jesus was born, three tall trees grew in the yard outside the stable: an olive tree, a date palm and a pine tree. To show how honoured they were to be growing beside the manger, the olive tree gave the baby a basketful of ripe olives and the palm tree gave him a great bunch of dates. The pine tree felt most upset. It had no gift for the baby so it drooped its branches almost to the ground with sadness. It was, as you will remember, a bright starry night and the stars, looking down, felt so sorry for the poor pine tree that they fell from the skies and landed on its dark evergreen branches. There they glistened and shone like jewels. The baby Jesus looked up and gurgled with laughter. It was the world's very first Christmas tree.

OBJECTIVES

To enable children to:
- learn that Christmas trees are evergreens (science)
- find out about the history and legends of the first Christmas tree (history).

OTHER CROSS-CURRICULAR LINKS

SCIENCE
Understanding the difference between evergreen and deciduous trees; recognising and naming some common evergreens.

ENGLISH
Writing poems about Christmas tree lights.

MUSIC
Learning the words and music of 'Oh, Christmas Tree'.

DESIGN AND TECHNOLOGY
Making stand-up Christmas trees.

ART AND DESIGN
Mixing paint to make different shades of green.

There is yet another story about how fir trees came to be part of our Christmas tradition. This story tells of a man called Martin Luther who lived in Germany in the sixteenth century. Nobody knows how true this story is but it might well have happened.

One winter night when Martin Luther was walking alone through the forest, he looked up and saw hundreds of stars shining through the branches of the trees. The scene made him think about the night that Jesus was born. 'I wish my children could see this!' he thought. So the next day he had a fir tree cut down and brought into his living room. The sharp smell of the forest filled the room. It was wonderful. Next, Martin Luther decorated the tree with candles to show the children how beautiful the stars had looked that night. When the children came into the living room and saw the tree alight with candles, they were thrilled. 'It's the most beautiful thing we have ever seen!' they said.

And ever since Martin Luther's time, fir trees have been brought into every home in Germany and decorated with lights for Christmas.

Tell the children that Prince Albert, Queen Victoria's husband, first introduced Christmas trees to Britain. In 1841 he bought a tree for his children. It was about eight feet tall and had wax tapers on the end of every branch. It was decorated with gingerbread men and egg shapes filled with sweets, all hung from brightly coloured ribbons.

Elicit from the children that wax tapers are candles. Ask why we no longer use candles to light Christmas trees and explain that we now use electric tree lights because they are much safer. Put some tree lights on an artificial tree, close the blinds and switch the lights on. Ask the children to suggest what they look like, for example *like lots of stars, like little flowers, like a shower of sparks* and so on. List these ideas on the board for later use.

Tell the children about the most famous Christmas tree in the world – the huge Norwegian spruce given each year by the people of Oslo in Norway to the city of London. The tree is always at least 21 metres high and over 50 years old. It is set up in Trafalgar Square and is lit with hundreds of white lights. Carols are sung beneath it and lots of people come to see it.

Differentiation

Ask good readers to look in the library for stories about Christmas trees, for example *The Little Crooked Christmas Tree* by Michael Cutting (Scholastic: Hippo). Arrange a stand-up display of illustrated Christmas tree story books. The children should 'catalogue' their finds on a word processor.

Now or later

■ Ask the children to write image poems about Christmas tree lights from the ideas already collected, for example:

Christmas lights
They twinkle like stars
in the night sky.
They are scattered like daisies
on the green grass.
They sparkle like jewels
on a dark dress.

Display the children's ideas as a group poem, written inside coloured baubles and strung together.

■ Play and sing 'Oh, Christmas Tree' and encourage the children to join in the chorus, *How evergreen your branches!* Then teach all the words and music of the song.

■ Discuss with the children why many people use artificial trees. The children can make stand-up Christmas trees from fine green card. They should fold an A5-sized card lengthways, then draw a half-tree outline along the fold. They can cut out the outline, then open out the shape. Ask them to cut a second tree shape to match. The first tree shape should then be cut from the top down to halfway and the second from the bottom up. The two outlines can be slotted together to make a tree that will stand up ready to be decorated with foil, tinsel and coloured paper.

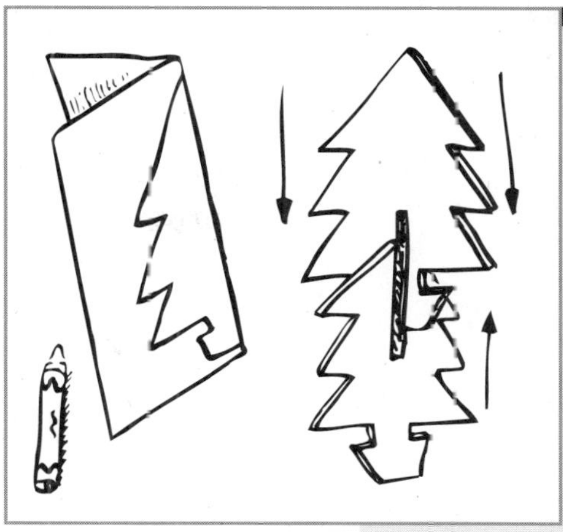

■ Encourage the children to look at the tree identification book and count how many different shades of green they can see. Ask them to mix paint (using green, blue, yellow and white) to match as many shades of green as possible. Make a large grid of squares and help the children fill each with a different green to make a wall of greens. This idea could be adapted to make unusual wrapping paper.

Carol-singing

Resources and classroom organisation

You will need: a piano or guitar and the music for a variety of Christmas carols, for example *Favourite Christmas Carols* by Charles Cafone (Dover Publications) or a tape player and cassette of recorded carols; an assortment of percussion instruments; pictures of carol-singers.

The children should work as a class beside the piano, guitar or tape player.

What to do

Ask the children to listen to one or two well-known carols played on tape or on an instrument, for example 'Away in a Manger', 'Once in Royal David's City', 'Silent Night'. Encourage them to join in with those carols with which they are already familiar. Then tell them about the history of carols:

A carol is a special song of joy and happiness. 'Carol' comes from the old French word 'carole', meaning a dance with a song. Long ago in England, carols were sung and danced to by farm workers and other country people to celebrate the shortest day of the year as they looked forward to the end of winter. 'Good King Wenceslas' is a good example of just such an old country song.

Gradually, carols began to be used in church services. A few years after Jesus died, the Pope wanted people to sing songs to celebrate Christmas. At first they were sung in Latin, so many ordinary people couldn't understand them.

It was St Francis of Assisi (in Italy) who decided to write carols in a language that people could understand. He brought an ox and an ass to the church where he was to celebrate the Christmas Mass to show people what it must have been like in the stable in Bethlehem. The people who came to this first Nativity service could hardly believe their eyes! They felt so happy afterwards that they walked home still singing, and that is how the custom of carol-singing in the streets is said to have started. The singing of carols using everyday words that were easy to understand soon spread around the world.

In England, carol singers used to be called 'wassail singers'. They went around their village, stopping at each house to sing a carol in return for cakes, mince pies and hot ale. Many people worked on farms and there was little work to be had in winter. Poor people were often hungry, so 'wassailing' around the doors of rich people was one way of getting some much-needed hot food and drink.

Objectives

To enable the children to:
■ find out about the history of carols and traditions associated with carol-singing (history)
■ become familiar with a number of traditional carols and learn to sing several new carols (music)
■ accompany the carols on percussion instruments (music).

Other cross-curricular links

Geography
Finding out about various carol-singing traditions in other countries.

Art and design
Creating a carol singers' frieze.

The wassailers had a special song to let people know they were on their way. They hoped that it would give them time to heat up ale or cider punch ready for their arrival. The song went like this:

Wassail! Wassail! All over the town,
Our toast is white, our ale is brown.
Our bowl it is made of the maplin tree,
We be good fellows. I drink to thee!

The wassailers, who were all men, would sing a few carols, then hold out their wooden wassail bowl which was decorated with evergreens and red ribbons. To show how much they had enjoyed the singing, the good people of the house would fill the wassailers' bowl with hot punch.

Then the women of the village thought that they too would go out carol-singing, so they carried a 'vessel-cup' from door to door. This was a little box, decorated with ribbons, containing small cut-out figures of the holy family standing on a bed of shredded paper. Just like the men, the women and children had their own favourite carol that told villagers they were on their way:

Here we come a-wassailing
Among the leaves so green.
Here we come a-carolling
So fair to be seen.
God send you happy! God send you happy
God send you all a happy New Year!

This is how the tradition of children going from house to house singing carols and wishing everyone a happy Christmas began.

There are many different carol-singing customs all over the world. In Germany and Austria children go carol-singing on the Thursday before Christmas. They sing at the tops of their voices and make a lot of noise, banging drums and blowing whistles. Sometimes they wear frightening masks and chase people down the street to frighten away the evil spirits of winter. Sometimes, the older boys push a hay fork round the doors and ask the people to put a Christmas bun on the end.

In Lapland, a carol service by candlelight takes place on the edge of the Arctic circle on the darkest night of the year. This must make a wonderful scene with all the candles flickering against the deep white snow.

In the United States, there is a tradition of 'Christmas tree choirs' when the singers dress in robes with bright white collars and arrange themselves in the shape of a giant Christmas tree.

In one part of Canada, it is traditional for people to sail across Vancouver harbour in brightly lit 'carol boats', so that their voices are heard from the shore and the lights are reflected in the water.

Today, in Britain, carol-singers still come round the doors, but more often, groups of singers gather around a Christmas tree in shopping centres or in busy streets. They usually collect money for hospitals or charities.

Show the children pictures of carol-singers and discuss how they are dressed – in warm coats, woollen mitts and hats, fur-lined boots and so on. Talk about how they might light their way with torches or lamps.

Finish the session by playing and singing some well-known carols. Encourage the children to join in by singing and playing percussion instruments.

Differentiation

Some of the children could make a model of a 'vessel-cup' using a shoe box. They can make stand-up cut-outs of the holy family figures and glue them to the floor of the box. Advise them to surround the figures with shredded coloured paper and decorate the box with ribbons. These vessel-cups can then be carried around the classrooms when the children go carol-singing.

Less able children could copy the first lines of carols using a word processor. These could be enlarged and made into banners to decorate the school hall during a carol service.

Now or later

- Help the children to learn some carols by heart so that they can go carol-singing for a Christmas assembly or at a church service, dressed up in bobble hats and scarves. Choose three or four carols and teach the words and music. If it is safe, the children could be given a nightlight on a saucer to carry in procession as they are singing.
- You might be able to organise a carol-singing session around the school, allowing the children to go singing from class to class. Suggest that they learn the wassailing songs to let everyone know they are on their way.
- Ask the children to find where Italy, Germany, Austria, the United States and Canada are on the map or globe of the world.
- Make a carol-singers frieze by asking each member of the class to paint the head and shoulders of a child, life-size. They should paint the face with an open mouth, as if he or she were singing and put a bright hat on each head and a scarf around the neck. When the painted faces are dry, ask the children to cut them out and glue them onto a dark background. Scatter some 'snow' across the 'choir' and add one or two lights or stars on sticks.

The Christingle service

Resources and classroom organisation

You will need: a candle to light in class; photocopiable page 48 and the materials to make Christingles; a Christingle already made; an oil lamp, torch, light bulb and so on.

The children should first work as a class, then in groups of about six.

Objectives

To enable children to:

- think about the importance of light in our everyday lives (science)
- consider how and why we use lights to help us celebrate Christmas (RE)
- think about children less fortunate than themselves (PSHE).

What to do

Introduce the activity by talking about the way we light our homes. Ask what lighting people used before electricity was discovered.

If possible, close the blinds and light a candle (emphasising the need for care). Encourage interesting vocabulary from the children to describe how the flame moves, for example *dancing, flickering, shining, glistening*. Introduce other forms of lighting, such as an oil lamp, fairy lights, and so on.

Discuss with the children how lights are used on various special occasions, for example, birthdays, parties, festivals of light, Diwali, church services and Bonfire Night.

OTHER CROSS-CURRICULAR LINKS

HISTORY

Learning about the history of domestic lighting, from candles to electricity.

ENGLISH

Using interesting vocabulary in oral work; writing poems about candle flames.

PE

Moving like flames.

Ask the children to suggest Christmas traditions where lights are used, for example fairy lights on Christmas trees, coloured lights in the streets and shop windows, stars used for decoration, candles on the Christmas cake, Christmas pudding being set alight, fireworks to celebrate New Year.

Find out if any of the children have been to a Christingle service and ask them what they remember about it. Explain that it is a special carol service in church or school where each child is given a Christingle with a candle in it. When all the Christingles are lit, the building is filled with candle-light. Toys or money are usually collected for less fortunate children. Tell the children that Christingle services were first held in Czechoslovakia over two hundred years ago and since then have been introduced into many other parts of the world.

Show a finished Christingle and explain that 'Christingle' means 'Christ light'. Pass the Christingle (unlit) around and tell the children that:

- the candle represents Jesus, light of the world
- the dried fruit is meant to make us think of good things to eat
- the four cocktail sticks represent the four seasons
- the red ribbon is to make us think of the blood of Christ.

Ask what they think the orange is intended to make us think about. (It is meant to be round as the Earth, round as the world.)

Then work with small groups of children to make Christingles following the instructions on photocopiable page 48.

NOW OR LATER

- Arrange and practise for a Christingle carol service. Let each child carry a lit candle in their Christingle. (Or, for absolute safety, the Christingles can remain unlit to be taken home later.) You could combine this with asking each child to bring a small, brightly wrapped toy for later distribution to a children's home or refugee centre.

- Suggest the children make up a Christingle dance, moving like flames. Encourage them to make flickering, twinkling, glittering, flaming movements.
- Ask the children to make pictures of Christingle candles with collage materials, using gold foil for the candle flames. Arrange the orange shapes on a bed of dark green cut-out holly leaves with red berries.
- Encourage the children to write poems about candles. They can use the writing pattern below or their own words.

Christmas candles
Dancing in the dark.
Flickering on the ___
Shining in the ___
Glistening on the ___

Pantomimes

Resources and classroom organisation

You will need: photocopiable pages 49 and 50 and the equipment and materials listed; a book of traditional stories, for example *The Illustrated Book of Fairy Tales* retold by Neil Philip (Dorling Kindersley); puppets of different kinds (string, hand, stick); a puppet theatre (or one devised from the play house or a covered table).

The children should work first as a class, then in small groups.

What to do

Talk with the children about all the special treats people enjoy at Christmas time, such as visiting Santa's grotto, going out for Christmas dinner, Christmas television, a visit to the theatre and so on. Share experiences of theatre visits with those that have been, for example being out late at night, the bright lights on stage, a story coming to life, the excitement that builds up among the audience and so on.

Find out if anyone has been to a Christmas pantomime and ask what it was like. Explain that in the first pantomimes, about 200 years ago in Britain, the stories were told without words, with actors using only mime and dance. The stories were always familiar, based sometimes on legends and fairy stories, sometimes on nursery rhymes. Gradually, words, songs and jokes were added to turn the stories into the Christmas pantomimes we enjoy today.

Discuss how the story often comes from a traditional tale, for example 'Dick Whittington' or 'Cinderella'. Talk about the traditions of men dressing up as women to play the 'dame' and girls dressing up as young men, the singing and dancing, audience participation and how everything is topsy-turvy but all turns out happily in the end.

Read the poem 'Look Behind You' on photocopiable page 49 and explore the pantomime themes with the children. Ask: *What is meant by 'Your head is full of stories'? What tells you that the child in the poem is still feeling excited when he or she gets home? What is happening when you call out 'Look behind you!' What story is being told when it says 'and Tinkerbell still flies'?*

Read and talk about a traditional story such as 'Cinderella'. Tell the children that the people who appear in the story are called 'characters'. Discuss the characters in the story you have chosen. For example, in 'Cinderella' there are five main characters – Cinderella, the two Ugly Sisters, the Prince, the Fairy Godmother – and lots of minor ones, such as coachmen, mice and people at the ball. Talk with the children about the kind of people these stock characters are. For example, Cinderella is *poor, overworked, sad, helpful* and so on while the Ugly Sisters are *spiteful, nasty, cruel* and so on.

Encourage the children to find 'voices' to go with these characters. Most children will enjoy this but take care not to push the more timid ones too hard. Get them to try out phrases that the 'goodies' or the 'baddies' in the story might say, such as *Get on with your work, girl! Wish a wish, my dear* or *I hope this glass slipper will fit.*

Encourage the children to put together some of these lines in an informal way, so that they can work on a puppet pantomime of the story. They should develop the tone of voice rather than be too concerned about the content.

Show the children the different puppets and how they can be made to move. Tell the children that together you are going to perform a pantomime using stick puppets and encourage them to think about how the characters can be dressed using scrap materials from the 'bits' box.

Organise the children into groups to make simple stick puppets, using photocopiable page 50.

Objectives

To enable children to:

- recognise that pantomimes follow a very traditional pattern (English)
- make a well-known story into a simple pantomime for a puppet theatre (English)
- make simple puppets (D&T)
- take part in a puppet play (English).

Other cross-curricular links

English
Understanding what is meant by a 'character' in a story, poem or play; exploring the poem 'Look Behind You!'.

History
Learning the background of pantomime tradition.

PE
Moving in dance as characters in a pantomime.

Differentiation
Independent writers could make a simple storyboard of the action. This could be developed into a wall story of the pantomime, with speech bubbles to show dialogue. Less able children could illustrate the wall story.

Now or later
- Let the children practise making the puppets move in the puppet theatre.
- When the pantomime is ready, ask the children to make tickets, produce a programme and so on and finally, put on an informal puppet performance for parents or another class to enjoy.
- In the hall, ask the children to mime, dance and sing like the pantomime characters in your favourite story.

Boxing Day

Objectives
To enable children to:
- look closely at a traditional carol to discover what it means (English)
- write their own version of the carol 'Good King Wenceslas' (English)
- find out about St Stephen's day and its traditions (history)
- find out about Boxing Day and Boxing Day traditions (history).

Other cross-curricular links
PSHE
Thinking about how important Boxing Day gifts used to be.

English
Writing a story from the words of Good King Wenceslas; getting to know the traditional mummer characters.

Art and design
Painting masks and designing costumes for the mummers; painting St Stephen's day scenes.

Resources and classroom organisation
You will need: a calendar; a recording of 'Good King Wenceslas' and a copy of the words to the carol; CD or cassette player; books about 'mummers' plays, for example *Discovering Christmas Customs and Folklore* by Margaret Baker (Shire Publications); A5 paper; adhesive tape; writing and drawing materials.

Organise the children all together to start with, then in their classroom places.

What to do
Show the children the month of December on the calendar and guide them towards Christmas Day, reinforcing the date. Tell them that, 26 December, the day after Christmas is called Boxing Day or St Stephen's Day.

Listen to 'Good King Wenceslas'. Ask if the children can work out the date on which King Wenceslas went out into the forest. Tell them that there is a clue in the song – *on the feast of Stephen.*

Read aloud the first verse, then ask the children questions about it, such as *Where was the king on that night? What was the weather like? Who did King Wenceslas meet?*

Explain that the king was a good Christian who tried to help everybody he met, so ask the children what they think might have happened next. Listen to their guesses before listening again to the words of the song on tape. Ask: *Who was trudging through the snow alongside the king? How did he feel about helping the poor man?* Point out how the king's page complained that the poor man's house was too far away to walk in the bitter wind. (A 'league' is a little over a mile.)

Ask the children what gifts the king took to the poor man's cottage. ('Flesh' or meat, wine and pine logs.) How do they think the poor man must have felt about Wenceslas who was rich and famous?

Explore the story as told in the song. Put the sequence of events on the board, like this perhaps: *The king went into the forest. It was snowing and very cold. He met a poor man gathering logs for the fire…* Elicit the 'bones' of the story from the children so that they can use the synopsis when writing their own versions later.

Tell the children that Boxing Day was named after an old tradition that used to take place on the day after Christmas:

> In Victorian times, rich people used to give presents to their servants and to local shopkeepers on the day after Christmas. These presents were called 'Christmas boxes' and that is how 26 December got its name. In some villages, boys went around collecting money in clay or earthenware boxes. When these were full, the boys broke open the boxes and shared out the pennies.

In one part of Austria, people bring their horses to be blessed in church on St Stephen's Day. They are given a special meal of salt, oats, bread and holy water in memory of St Stephen who loved horses and had seven of his own.

In some English villages, for example Marshfield in South Gloucester, mumming is a Boxing Day tradition that lots of people look forward to. Mumming is a street performance of an ancient folk play that usually takes place on Boxing Day morning. The words are the same each year and so are all the characters – St George and the Dragon, the King, the Knight, Father Christmas and the Doctor. In Marshfield, Father Christmas always says:

In comes I, old Father Christmas,
Welcome or welcome not.
I hope old Father Christmas
Will never be forgot.

To finish the activity, listen again to the tape of 'Good King Wenceslas' and read over the story synopsis from the board. Ask the children to write out their own version of the story, using A5 sheets, taped together to make a zigzag book. The children can illustrate the story on each double-page spread.

Differentiation

Independent writers can try making up fun rhymes for the other characters who take part in the mummers' play, such as St George, the Doctor and the Dragon. Each verse should begin, *Here comes I...* These don't need to make a lot of sense but they must rhyme, for example:

Here comes I
a dragon bold.
Listen to my story
which must be told.

Or

Here comes I
a dragon bold.
My spikes are green,
my eyes are gold.

Ask the children to speak their rhymes and present their own mummer mask play.

Less able children might enjoy drawing boys breaking the clay boxes with the pennies dropping to the ground. They could represent the pennies with gold paper.

Now or later

- The children might like to find out more about mumming from, for example, *Discovering Christmas Customs and Folklore* by Margaret Baker. They could then draw the mummers from photographs, paying special attention to their traditional costumes.
- Ask the children to make paper plate masks for the characters in the mummers' play. Explain that they usually had fearsome faces and straggly hair. The children could make the hair with scraps of wool and tape a plant stick to the back of the mask.
- Ask the children to draw a picture of the horses waiting outside the church to be blessed on St Stephen's Day. Remind them to show the oats, salt, bread and water.
- Working in groups, ask the children to paint a frieze of the snowy forest scene 'on the feast of Stephen'. They should use only white, black, blue and brown to paint a cold landscape scene in the middle of a dark night. Ask them to think about pale night-time colours and the silence of a snowy forest to give the picture a mysterious feeling. They may wish to add a yellow Moon and stars.

Name Date

Make your own Christingle

You will need:

1 orange
red ribbon
a mapping pin
a piece of foil (about 20×20cm)
a candle
4 cocktail sticks
some dried fruits (sultanas, raisins, glace cherries, for example)

What to do:

1. Carefully make a hole in the orange for the candle (for example with an apple corer).
2. Put some red ribbon around the orange and fasten it with a mapping pin.
3. Place a square of foil around the base of the candle and squeeze it into shape. This will collect the candle wax safely.
4. Put the candle into the hole in the orange and make sure it is upright.
5. Stick four cocktail sticks into the orange.
6. Thread sultanas, raisins or glace cherries onto the sticks.

Name Date

Look behind you!

Your head is full of stories,
eyes filled with light.
It's the magic of the pantomine
and you're out late at night.

You sit between your mum and dad,
laughing and calling out,
"Watch out! Look behind you!"
and nobody minds if you shout!

It's very odd, the men wear skirts
and make a lot of jokes.
Even odder, girls in spangled tights
pretend to be skinny blokes.

Everything is painted bright colours,
the sky and the village street.
And everyone is supposed to sing when
they show you words on a sheet.

When the pantomine ends, music plays on
and Tinkerbell still flies,
the story replays inside your head and
stars sparkle on in your eyes.

Moira Andrew

Name Date

Make a stick puppet

1. Cut out the figure on this sheet. Then draw around it on a piece of card and cut that out.

2. Draw a face on your puppet and use wool to make some hair.

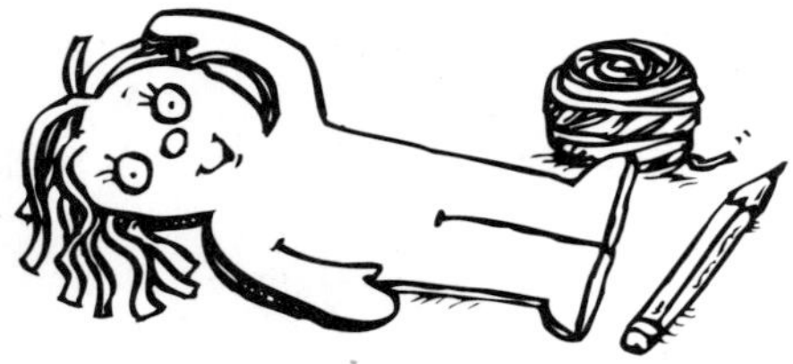

3. Make clothes with bits of material and coloured paper.

4. Use sticky tape to fix a stick to the back of your puppet.

Your puppet is now ready to perform!

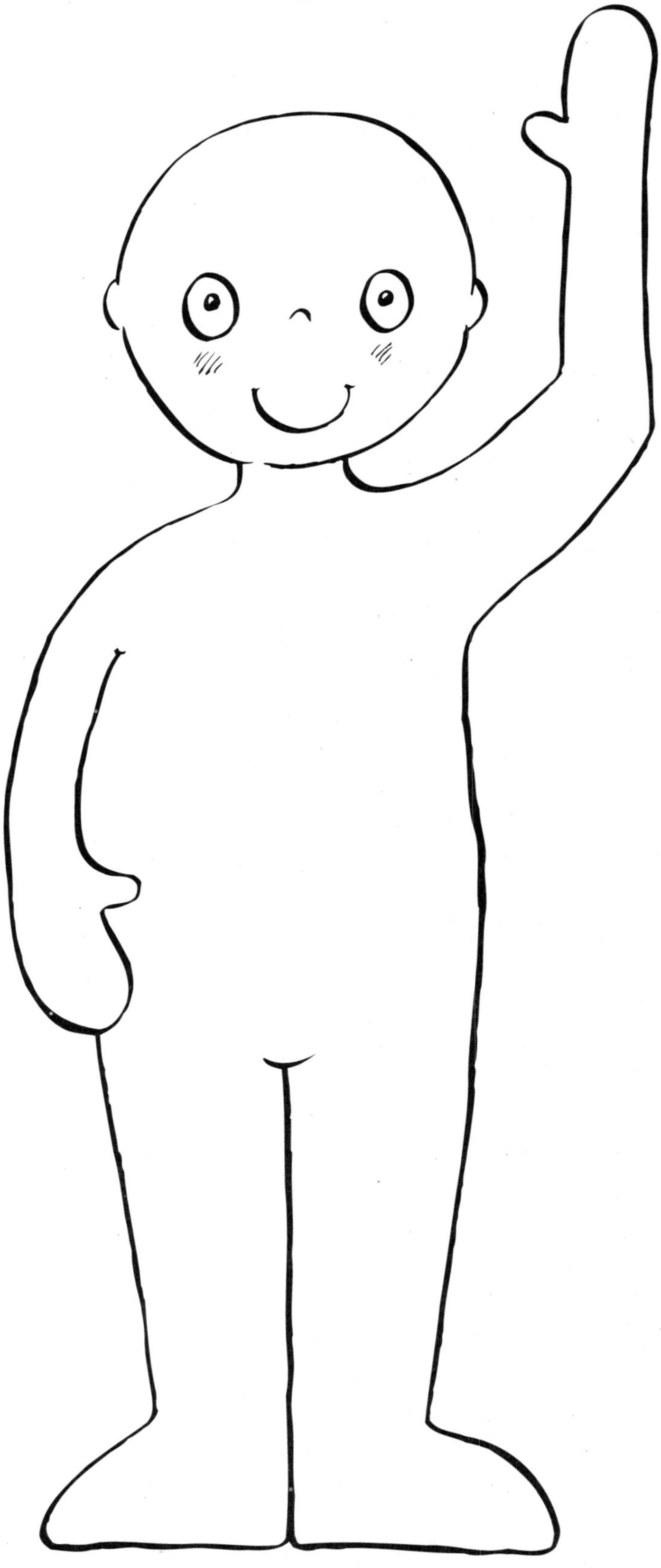

Section 6

Feasting and jollity

This section explores the ways in which people enjoy themselves during the Christmas festival. It also encourages children to think about the importance of sharing with others and celebrating with friends and family.

Christmas food

Resources and classroom organisation

You will need: a map of Europe; photocopiable page 59 and the ingredients and equipment to make Lebkuchen.

Begin with the children seated in a class, then divide the class into small groups.

What to do

Tell the children that we call Christmas the 'festive season' and remind them that Christmas is just one of the festivals that we celebrate throughout the year, for example Easter, Diwali, Hanukkah, Harvest Festival and so on. Discuss how we sometimes eat different foods from usual during our particular festivals.

Talk about the special food we might have at Christmas time to help us celebrate – turkey, mince pies, trifle, Christmas pudding and so on. Let the children look through the magazines and recipe books to find pictures of food they look forward to eating at Christmas time. Ask the children to suggest how the dinner table will be decorated – with candles, sprigs of holly, crackers and so on. Share their anticipation and excitement.

Discuss what plum or Christmas pudding looks like and its main ingredients, for example dried fruit, flour, suet, sugar and sometimes, brandy (see 'Stir-up Sunday' on page 5 and photocopiable page 11).

Ask the children to listen to this story called 'The King's Christmas pudding' which suggests how plum pudding was invented. (First discuss with the children what a legend is and explain that this story is an old English legend.)

One cold Christmas Eve the King went riding through the forest. He was all alone. The snow began to fall, drifting like soft feathers at first, then faster and faster until the King was lost in a white world of whirling snowflakes.

It grew late and night closed in, making the snowy forest an eerie place to be. The trees became dark shadows murmuring under their caps of snow and the King, shivering with cold, started to feel very hungry.

Then he saw lights in a woodcutter's cottage so he knocked on the door.

'Please help me,' he said. 'I'm frozen to the bone and extremely hungry.'

The woodcutter invited the King to come inside and sit by the fire. He was very poor and could find little for the King to eat.

'I'm sorry, sire,' he said. 'My larder is almost empty. All I can find is a little flour, some sugar and dried currants.'

The King searched his bag and said, 'And all I can find is a half-bottle of brandy.'

So they decided to share what they had. They mixed everything together and put the sweet sticky mixture into a bag. Then they boiled it up over the fire.

When it was ready, the King and the woodcutter sat down to a delicious feast, unaware that they were enjoying the first-ever Christmas pudding!

Objectives

To enable children to:
- appreciate that special foods are an important part of celebrations (RE)
- read and follow recipes (English)
- appreciate that not everyone has enough to eat (PSHE)
- make biscuits (D&T).

Other cross-curricular links

RE
Thinking about sharing.

PSHE
Understanding the importance of hygiene in the kitchen; cooking Christmas 'goodies'.

English
Looking at a legend; writing about favourite foods; writing Christmas-pudding poems.

Design and technology
Gift-packaging home-made sweets.

Give the children a chance to think about the story, then ask if there are parts of it that make them think it is a legend rather than a true story. For example, a king visiting a woodcutter; the only food in the house being this strange combination of ingredients.

Talk about how much we tend to eat at Christmas. Often we are too full up to eat any Christmas pudding at the end of the Christmas meal. Explore the idea that not everyone is as lucky as we are. Many people, particularly in poor countries, don't ever have enough food to eat, not even on Christmas Day.

Tell the children that in our own country, in days of old, many people and their animals often went hungry during the cold winter months. Most of the corn and hay stored for the animals had been used up, so the animals were killed for food. This meant that the people could look forward to having a huge feast of meat at Christmas.

Just as we do today, everyone tried to make their Christmas meal very special in order to brighten up the darkest days of winter. Instead of turkey, people often had peacocks, roast goose or sometimes a whole roasted pig for Christmas dinner. They usually followed this with plum pudding and mince pies and finished off with nuts and sweets.

Point out that people in other countries celebrate Christmas with different kinds of food. Read about some of the special Christmas treats served in different places across Europe (show where these countries are on the map as you read):

- In Scandinavia, they eat lots of fish for Christmas – herring, dried cod or stewed eels – because fish is a great treat for them.
- In Austria, they have special pork sausages.
- In Denmark and Sweden, they begin their meal with porridge or rice pudding with one almond hidden inside. The person who finds the nut gets a prize. In Denmark, it's usually a marzipan pig.
- In Belgium, the shops are full of fancy biscuits and they have cakes and bread marked with a cross.
- In France, they have a special Christmas treat called *buche de Noel*, which is a cake shaped like a log and made with crushed chestnuts.
- In Greece, a *Christopsomo* Christmas loaf is baked on Christmas Eve. The first slice is usually given to some poor person who hasn't enough to eat. Another special treat to eat in Greece at Christmas is liver!
- In Italy, the Christmas cake is called *pannetone*. It is baked with candied peel and sultanas and is so rich that one small slice is usually enough.
- In Germany, the children look forward to *Lebkuchen* ginger biscuits. They are cut into the shape of hearts, stars, trees, houses and so on, threaded with ribbons and hung from the Christmas tree.

Suggest that the children can make Lebkuchen to put on their tree at home. Read the recipe on photocopiable page 59 with the children and gather the necessary ingredients.

Divide the children into groups (with adult support) to bake the biscuits. Use Christmas cutters to make them into appropriate shapes. Thread them with ribbon ready to hang from the tree and let every child have one to take home.

Now or later

- Make a floor book from the magazine cuttings of the children's favourite Christmas food, encouraging individuals to write a few lines about why they have chosen their favourite.
- Ask the children to write a Christmas-pudding poem in about four lines. The poems can be displayed inside a circle, coloured brown with dark splodges for currants and decorated with a sprig of holly on top.
- Talk about cooking and baking and the care we need to take in the kitchen. Write some simple rules of hygiene on the board.
- With adult help, groups of children can look for recipes of and make simple non-cook sweets, such as almond delights.

■ Encourage the children to find attractive ways to wrap sweets (home-made or shop-bought) in foil and coloured tissue paper or old Christmas wrapping paper. They can decorate these sweets with scraps of tinsel or ribbon and take them home as gifts for their families or friends.

Christmas parties

Resources and classroom organisation

You will need: photocopiable pages 60–2, enlarged or on OHT for display, and the ingredients and equipment detailed; cups and ingredients to make up drinks (clear lemonade, cola, fruit juices, slices of lemon, ice cubes and so on).

The children should sit together as a class, then divide into groups (with adult support) to make pizzas.

What to do

Talk about parties that are held to celebrate Christmas, for example at school, at clubs like Beavers or Brownies and at home. Encourage the children to describe parties they have enjoyed, including party food, games, prizes, party hats and so on.

Read and discuss the poem, 'The Christmas Party' on photocopiable page 60, then ask the children to retell the story of the poem. Ask them: *Why wasn't Dad looking forward to the party? Who did most of the preparation? What did the child in the poem worry about before the party?*

Help the children to comment on the pattern of the poem. Encourage them to notice the last line of each verse – *they said, Mum said, Dad said* and so on. Ask them to suggest alternatives, for example *Dad groaned, asked, everyone shouted.*

Draw the children's attention to the speech marks and ask them to find some of the words people said. Encourage them to make up new dialogue for each of the characters in the poem. They might also like to invent new characters for the party. Ask the children whether they think it was a successful party or a disaster and to explain their answers.

Explain to the children that, a long time ago, parties were mostly for adults rather than children. Tell them about the history of Christmas parties:

Objectives

To enable children to:
- find out about the history of games traditionally played at Christmas parties (history)
- read and discuss a pattern poem (English)
- design and write party games and invitations (English)
- plan a Christmas party programme (D&T).

Other cross-curricular links

Design and technology
Decorating balloons, making crackers; making party drinks and pizzas.

PSHE
Thinking of others.

Art and design
Designing invitations.

English
Recognising how speech marks are used to denote dialogue; creating dialogue and characters.

Christmas is usually a time for fun and games and special food. In years gone by, people did not have much time during the year to go to parties and enjoy themselves because they were too busy working. Also, there were laws that said people were not allowed to make too much noise or play gambling games except during the twelve days of Christmas. It was then that people could really relax and enjoy the Christmas celebrations, singing, dancing and playing games.

In big houses, one of the servants was often chosen to be the Lord of Misrule for the twelve days of Christmas. It was his job to organise parties, plays, dances and pantomimes. Sometimes he ordered great firework displays to take place in the gardens, much to the delight of the children of the house. People had a wonderful time, eating lots of rich food, dancing, making music, singing carols and playing games.

Sometimes the children 'ducked' or dived for apples in a tub of water or tried to take a bite of treacle-covered buns hanging from a string above their heads. They also played games like those we play today such as 'Musical chairs', 'Hunt the slipper' and 'Blind man's buff'.

Encourage discussion about party games the children play nowadays. Ask those children who know any of the old-fashioned games to explain the rules to the others. The children can also make up a set of rules for their favourite game. From their explanations, write some rules on the board, keeping them as simple as possible. Demonstrate how rules for a game are easier to follow if they are numbered.

Suggest to the children that together they plan a Christmas party. Write up a list of their ideas, for example food, drinks, party hats, decorations, games to play and so on.

Elicit the idea of writing and sending invitations. Show the children some examples of party invitations and photocopiable page 61. Look at the pattern of each with them and point out that the place, date and time of the party are important. Now ask the children to fill in the details for the school Christmas party on their own copies of the photocopiable sheet.

Then ask the children to make up an ideal party menu, not forgetting savoury foods, such as pizzas, sausages on sticks, cheese dips.

Discuss the children's favourite party drinks. Provide simple ingredients such as clear lemonade, cola, fruit juice, slices of lemon and ice cubes and let the children invent new party drinks. They can give them exciting names like *Cola cooler, Jazzy juice, Lemon fizzer or Christmas chiller*. Organise a 'blind tasting' to show how an unusual name can make a simple drink seem more inviting.

List a games plan for the party, with the children working out what is needed for each game. For example, music and a prize wrapped in layers of paper for 'Pass the parcel'; a blindfold, a picture of the stable scene, a cut-out star and a pin for 'Pin the star above the stable'.

Ask the children to suggest decorations for the Christmas party, ranging from paper chains to personalised balloons and home-made crackers. You might like to tell the children how crackers were invented:

A man called Tom Smith invented crackers in 1847. The story goes that he was sitting in front of his fire one winter's night eating from a bowl of wrapped sweets.

Tom didn't have a lot of money and he was wondering how to give his children something special for Christmas. He was idly twiddling with the sweet wrappers when he had an idea.

'If I wrap up a paper hat and small present in a tube of coloured paper, I can make it look like a huge boiled sweet. That will surprise the children!' he thought. So he set to work.

He made a fancy paper hat, wrote out a riddle and found a tiny present for each child. Then he wrapped them all in coloured paper and decorated them with ribbons.

For a special surprise, Tom added a friction strip to make the crackers go pop when they were opened. It took him all night.

Then he put one of his 'crackers' at each child's place ready for the Christmas meal.

The children were delighted with their crackers. They asked him to make some for their friends. Soon everyone wanted crackers for their parties, so Tom Smith began to make them in a factory. His crackers became very famous and a 'must' at every children's party, especially at Christmas time.

Finish the session by demonstrating how easy it is to make a pizza for a party using a shop-bought base. Choose two children to be cooks, making sure that they first wash their hands. Display the recipe on photocopiable page 62, then follow it step by step, with the cooks organising the ingredients and showing the others what to do.

Divide the children into groups (with adult support) to let them make their own pizzas, devising different toppings.

Differentiation

Independent writers can write out recipes for some of the newly-invented drinks as above. Less able children can draw step-by-step instructions for pizzas using shop-bought bases. They should number the steps.

Now or later

■ Ask the children to write invitations to a 'pizza party' on A5 pieces of card. They could invite parents, governors or children from another class. Encourage them to put coloured Christmas borders around each invitation.

■ Organise the children to make crackers using a long cardboard tube (from kitchen towel or cling film, for example) as a base. They will need to hide a small packet of sweets or similar inside each tube before covering it with crêpe paper (overlapping at each end) and making it into a Christmas figure such as Father Christmas or one of the Three Kings. They can make a head and arms to glue into place. Finally, the ends of each cracker will need to be tied with ribbon or Christmas string.

■ Let the children decorate balloons for their party. An adult will need to blow up a balloon for each child and tie it to a string. The children can use gummed paper (or just cut paper and glue it) to make a funny face on each balloon. They might choose to make a Father Christmas face with white cotton wool whiskers. They could use scraps of wool glued on top to make hair. Tie a label to the string with the child's name on it.

■ Ask the children to make party hats using crêpe paper. Each child will need to cut a strip of paper to fit around its head, then staple or glue the two ends together. They can snip triangular pieces from it to make a crown and decorate it with sticky stars or motifs from old Christmas wrapping paper.

Lights and candles

Objectives

To enable children to:

■ consider how candles are used in celebrations (RE)

■ appreciate that candles are used by Christians to symbolise Jesus as 'the light of the world' (RE)

■ learn why candles are used in Christmas celebrations (history)

■ make a candle wax resist picture (A&D)

Resources and classroom organisation

You will need: various lights (or pictures of them) including torch, electric light, oil lamp; a collection of candles and candle-holders (including birthday candles, night-lights and so on); safety matches; candle snuffer; three different-sized jars; wax crayons; white paper; paint; scissors; glue, gold foil; card.

The children should work as a class to begin with, then break into groups for activities.

What to do

Close the blinds. When the children become accustomed to the darkness, ask them to think of ways of bringing light into the room. Look at and discuss electric lights, lamps, candles and so on. Talk about other kinds of lights and their importance, for example traffic lights, Christmas tree lights, lighthouses and the Sun.

Light a candle. Ask the children to notice how it makes a single point of bright light in the gloom and to watch how the flame flickers and dances. Then switch on the room light and ask what appears to happen to the candle-light: *You can't see it so well. It almost disappears,* and so on. Discuss why this is so.

OTHER CROSS-CURRICULAR LINKS

HISTORY

Learning about the pagan worship of fire and Sun; making a timeline to show the history of lights.

SCIENCE

Examining light in various forms; exploring the way a lit candle responds to loss of air.

ENGLISH

Using interesting vocabulary to describe candle-light and sunlight; composing poems about fire, Sun, candles.

Open the blinds, blow out the candle and encourage the children to consider why light plays such an important part in our lives. Answers may range from *It lets us see where we are going* to more profound statements like *Light helps things to grow*. Tell the children that Christians talk about Jesus as 'the light of the world' because that helps people understand how important they believe him to be. When they light candles at Christmas it makes them think of Jesus coming like 'a light into a dark world.' Prepare the children to listen to a story:

> Long ago, before Jesus was born, people worshipped the Sun because they knew that it brought the light they needed to stay alive.
>
> On the shortest day of the year, people built huge bonfires which they thought would give the Sun strength to come back into the skies. Then, at the end of December, when the days began to lengthen, the people rejoiced because they knew that spring was on its way. It was a time for feasting and singing and dancing. They lit lamps and candles and built great log fires in the hearth.
>
> After the birth of Jesus, Christians started to light candles to celebrate. They lit the four candles for Advent, candles on the Christmas tree, candles on St Lucy's crown, candles for each of the twelve days of Christmas, and in churches, carols were sung by candle-light.

Discuss with the children other times of the year when we use candles in our celebrations, for example birthdays, anniversaries, Diwali and Hanukkah.

Once again, close the blinds and light a candle. Ask the children to observe the movement of the flame and to describe it – *swaying, flickering, fluttering* and so on. As the candle burns away, encourage the children to suggest words to describe that, such as *dying, melting, shrinking*. Write some of this interesting vocabulary on the board.

Tell the children how Christmas trees used to be lit by candles, not by electric lights as they are today. Discuss what makes candles dangerous and ask the children to suggest safe places in which to stand a candle, for example in a candlestick, foil case or birthday candle holder.

Investigate ways in which a candle can be extinguished, starting with the most obvious means, letting a child carefully blow it out. Then demonstrate the use of a snuffer and explain that candles need air to burn. Let the children see what happens to the flames of three night lights when they are put under three different-sized jars.

Ask the children to make Christmas cards with wax resist candle pictures on the front. Let them experiment using wax crayons to make lines, loops, zigzags and other designs on a sheet of white paper. They will need to lean heavily on the crayons. They can then 'wash' the paper with thin paint and the wax will 'resist' it to make the patterns appear through the paint.

When the paint is dry, help the children to cut a fat candle shape from their sheet of paper. This candle can then be topped with a gold foil flame and used as decoration for the front of a Christmas card.

DIFFERENTIATION

Ask independent writers to write a factual account of what happens to a candle when the air is shut out.

Children needing more support could draw a Christmas street scene with as many different lights as they can think of, including street lights, car headlights, shop window lights, Christmas lights and so on.

Now or later

■ Encourage the children to use the vocabulary words collected earlier to make a pattern poem describing candle flames, for example:

A Christmas candle
Flickering and dancing,
swaying and fluttering
till it shrinks and dies
as it runs out of breath.

■ The children can make up similar poems about fire or the Sun using more of the words from the list, for example:

Fire is red as blood.
It sparkles and dances,
glowing with flames
on cold Christmas nights.

The Sun is like a balloon
floating in the air.
It is like a hula-hoop
rolling across the sky.

■ Make a 'timeline' of lights with the children, beginning with candles and oil lamps through to electric lights and lasers.

Family and guests

Objectives

To enable children to:
■ understand that Christmas is primarily a family occasion (PSHE/RE)
■ remember the old and the lonely who may be unable to share in Christmas celebrations (PSHE)
■ make a Christmas table decoration (D&T).

Resources and classroom organisation

You will need: photocopiable page 63 and the materials detailed; *Lucy and Tom's Christmas* by Shirley Hughes (Puffin Books) or another book with a similar family theme.

Work with the children as a whole class.

What to do

Discuss with the children what usually makes the Christmas meal different from others throughout the year, for example *Special food like turkey and mince pies, Aunts and uncles and grannies come, We play games after, We have decorations on the table, There are presents and crackers.* Note their ideas on the board.

Take time to listen to the children's memories and expectations, being aware of and playing down possible family problems or friction.

Talk about the tradition of family and friends gathering at Christmas and sharing a special Christmas meal. Tell them that a few hundred years ago, the meals often lasted all day! It can be the only time of year when family members meet up so there is a lot of catching up to do. It is usually a time for fun and laughter.

Point out to the children that when we are enjoying Christmas dinner, it is important to remember old, lonely or homeless people who have no family with whom to share this special time. Tell the children that in the Czech and Slovak Republics there is a tradition of leaving an empty place at the table in case Jesus should come to call. It is called 'Christ's chair'. Sometimes, a homeless person is invited in to sit in the chair and share the feast.

In Austria, when the family goes off to church, they leave the table set for their Christmas meal and always put out a jug of milk for Mary and the baby Jesus.

Remind the children that not everyone has a holiday on Christmas Day. Discuss all the people that have to work very hard on Christmas Day, for example parents cooking dinner, doctors and nurses in hospital, the electricity people, the police and so on.

Remind the children to say *Thank you* to the people at home who have worked to make the Christmas dinner a success and encourage them to offer to help clear away and wash up.

Talk with the children about how different and special the Christmas table looks and suggest ways in which they can help make table decorations and place cards. Encourage them to offer some of their own ideas and sketch or write them on the board.

With the children's help, demonstrate how to put together a festive spice tree (see photocopiable page 63) to make a table centre for the school dining hall. The children could take home their copy of the instructions to make a table centre for their own Christmas dinner table.

Finish the session by reading Shirley Hughes's *Lucy and Tom's Christmas* or another book with a similar family theme.

Other cross-curricular links

Design and technology
Designing and making place cards; making letter biscuits.

RE
Looking at the tradition of 'Christ's place' or empty chair at the Christmas dinner table.

PSHE
Appreciating those whose hard work has made the Christmas meal possible.

History
Making a family tree.

English
Writing about family memories of 'the best-ever Christmas'.

Now or later

- Suggest that the children ask at home about family relationships, thinking especially about those who have been invited to the Christmas meal. If it is possible (bearing in mind complications of stepfamilies and so on), help the children to make a simple three-generation family tree in the shape of a Christmas tree.
- Encourage the children to ask relatives and friends to tell them about their best-ever Christmas. They could tape-record the answers and these could be transcribed into a 'Memories of Christmas' class book.
- Working from their ideas on the board, invite the children to make place cards from pieces of folded A5 card for the guests invited to their own Christmas meals. Encourage them to use the names they themselves use, for example *Grandma, Gramps, Auntie Rose, Granny Thompson* and so on. The place cards can be decorated with felt-tipped pens and scraps of ribbon and tinsel.
- With adult supervision, the children could make St Nicholas letter biscuits of their dinner guests' initials to use as unusual 'place cards'.

Name Date

Lebkuchen

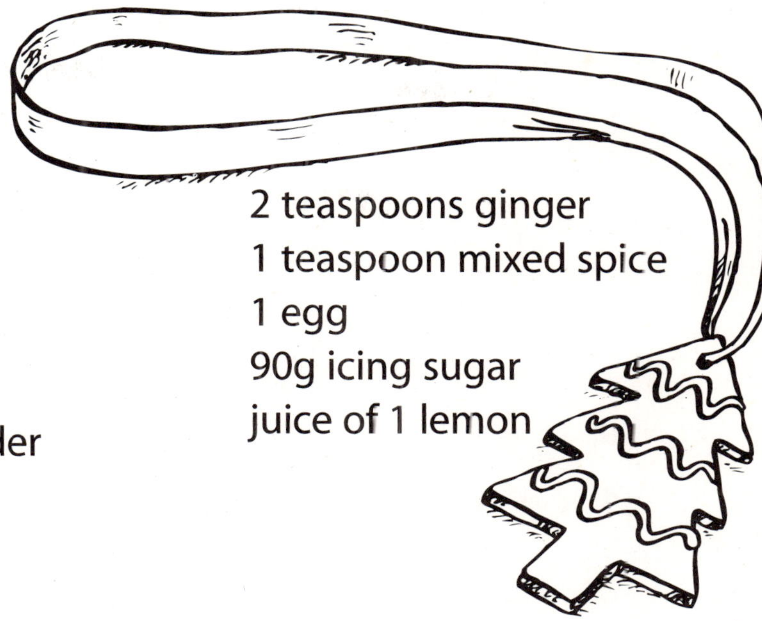

Ingredients:

4 tablespoons honey
60g margarine
60g brown sugar
250g plain flour
1 teaspoon baking powder
30g cocoa powder
2 teaspoons ginger
1 teaspoon mixed spice
1 egg
90g icing sugar
juice of 1 lemon

What to do:

1. Set the oven to 200°C.
2. Melt the honey, brown sugar and margarine in a pan. Leave to cool.
3. Sieve the flour, baking powder, cocoa and spices into a bowl. Add the egg yolk. (Put the egg white aside.)
4. Using a metal spoon, mix the warm honey mixture into the flour. Then squeeze the mixture into a ball.
5. Roll the dough out on a floured board until it is just thicker than a pound coin.
6. Use a pastry cutter to cut shapes from the dough. Make a hole in the top of each biscuit using a skewer.
7. Place the biscuits on a greased baking tray and bake for about 10 minutes.
8. Let the biscuits cool on a wire tray.
9. Sieve the icing sugar into a bowl. Slowly add 2 teaspoons of egg white and a few drops of lemon juice to make the icing.
10. Spoon some icing into an icing bag and make squiggly patterns over the biscuits.
11. When the icing is set, thread ribbons through the top of the Lebkuchen and hang them on the Christmas tree.

Name Date

The Christmas party

I sent out lots of invitations
on paper with balloons on.
Please come to my party,
they said.

For days on end, we all
thought about party food.
"Pizzas, sausage rolls, pop..."
Mum said.

Dad wasn't too keen.
"All these kids! Not a chance
of football on the box!"
Dad said.

I worried about it too.
What to do? What to wear?
"Will Granny want to kiss me?"
I said.

Saturday. My whole class came.
We ate everything in sight
and Jason was sick. "Sorry,"
he said.

I was the coolest kid in town,
and Granny didn't kiss me.
"Great music! Great party!"
everyone said.

Mum looked at the mess
and sighed. "I'm glad Christmas
comes just once a year!"
she said.

Moira Andrew

Name Date

Party invitation

Name Date

Simple pizzas

Ingredients:

4 small pizza bases
250g jar of tomato paste
100g grated cheese
slices of mushrooms
or cold cooked sausage

What to do:

1. Heat the oven to 200°C.

2. Put the bases on a baking tray.

3. Spread the tomato paste over the pizza bases and sprinkle on the grated cheese.

4. Add the mushroom slices or the sausage slices.

5. Put the pizzas in the oven for about 8 minutes until the cheese has melted. (Remember to use oven gloves.)

Name Date

Festive spice tree

You will need:

floral foam
a foil or terracotta saucer
sprigs of yew or fir
bits of holly
fine wire
ribbon or tinsel bows
cinnamon sticks,
vanilla pods, citrus peel,
nutmegs, cloves
satsumas

What to do:

1. Put a piece of floral foam in the saucer and wet it quite well.

2. Stick sprigs of yew, fir and holly into the foam. Make it into a tree shape.

3. Wire together the cinnamon sticks, vanilla pods, citrus peel and other spices. Push these 'spice kebabs' into the foliage.

4. Decorate with red or silver bows.

5. Put tangerines around the finished spice tree.

You now have a lovely, spicy smelling decoration for the dinner table.

Skills Grid

NATIONAL STANDARDS FOR KEY SKILLS

	English	RE	Art and design	Design and technology	History	PSHE	Science	Geography	PE	Music	Dance	Maths
Stir-up Sunday	✔	✔	✔		✔			✔				
Getting ready for Christmas	✔	✔	✔	✔	✔	✔						
Winter weather		✔	✔		✔		✔		✔			
The journey to Bethlehem	✔	✔			✔	✔		✔				
The first Christmas	✔	✔	✔		✔	✔					✔	
The Little Fir Tree	✔			✔		✔	✔					
The legend of the spider's web	✔	✔	✔	✔		✔	✔					✔
The birds' Christmas tree	✔		✔	✔		✔	✔					✔
The Twelve Days of Christmas	✔	✔	✔		✔		✔			✔		
Jingle Bells	✔	✔	✔				✔		✔	✔		
The Christmas Star	✔	✔		✔	✔		✔	✔			✔	
Away in a Manger	✔	✔	✔			✔				✔	✔	
Father Christmas or Santa Claus?	✔	✔		✔	✔	✔		✔				
St Lucy's Day		✔		✔	✔	✔		✔				
Christkind			✔	✔	✔	✔						
Christmas trees	✔		✔	✔	✔		✔			✔		
Carol-singing		✔	✔		✔			✔		✔		
The Christingle service	✔	✔			✔	✔	✔		✔			
Pantomimes	✔			✔	✔				✔		✔	
Boxing Day	✔		✔		✔	✔					✔	
Christmas food	✔	✔		✔		✔						
Christmas parties	✔		✔	✔		✔						
Lights and candles	✔	✔	✔		✔		✔					
Family and guests	✔	✔		✔	✔	✔						